DIESEL

live fast

STUNNING advertising

publicidad de impacto

monsa

Stunning Advertising
Publicidad de Impacto

Editor
Josep Mª Minguet

Author / Autor
Design & Layout / Diseño & Maquetación
Eva Minguet Cámara
Euipo editorial Monsa

Translation / Traducción
Babyl Traducciones

© INSTITUTO MONSA DE EDICIONES
Gravina, 43
08930 Sant Adrià de Besòs
Barcelona
España
Tlf. +34 93 381 00 50
Fax +34 93 381 00 93
www.monsa.com
monsa@monsa.com

ISBN 10 84-96823-30-X
ISBN 13 978-84-96823-30-3

Pictured L to R: If you're reading this, you really need to see Linda McCartney's Sixties: Portrait of an Era. December 1 through January 31.

ROYAL BC MUSEUM

monsa

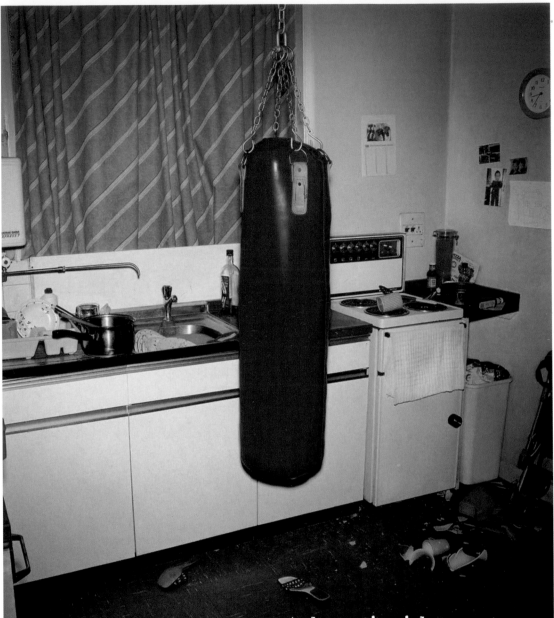

A domestic violence
victim will be beaten 20 times
in the next year,
unless a friend stops it sooner.

Call the National Domestic Violence Helpline for support.

Helpline run by Refuge and Women's Aid

index

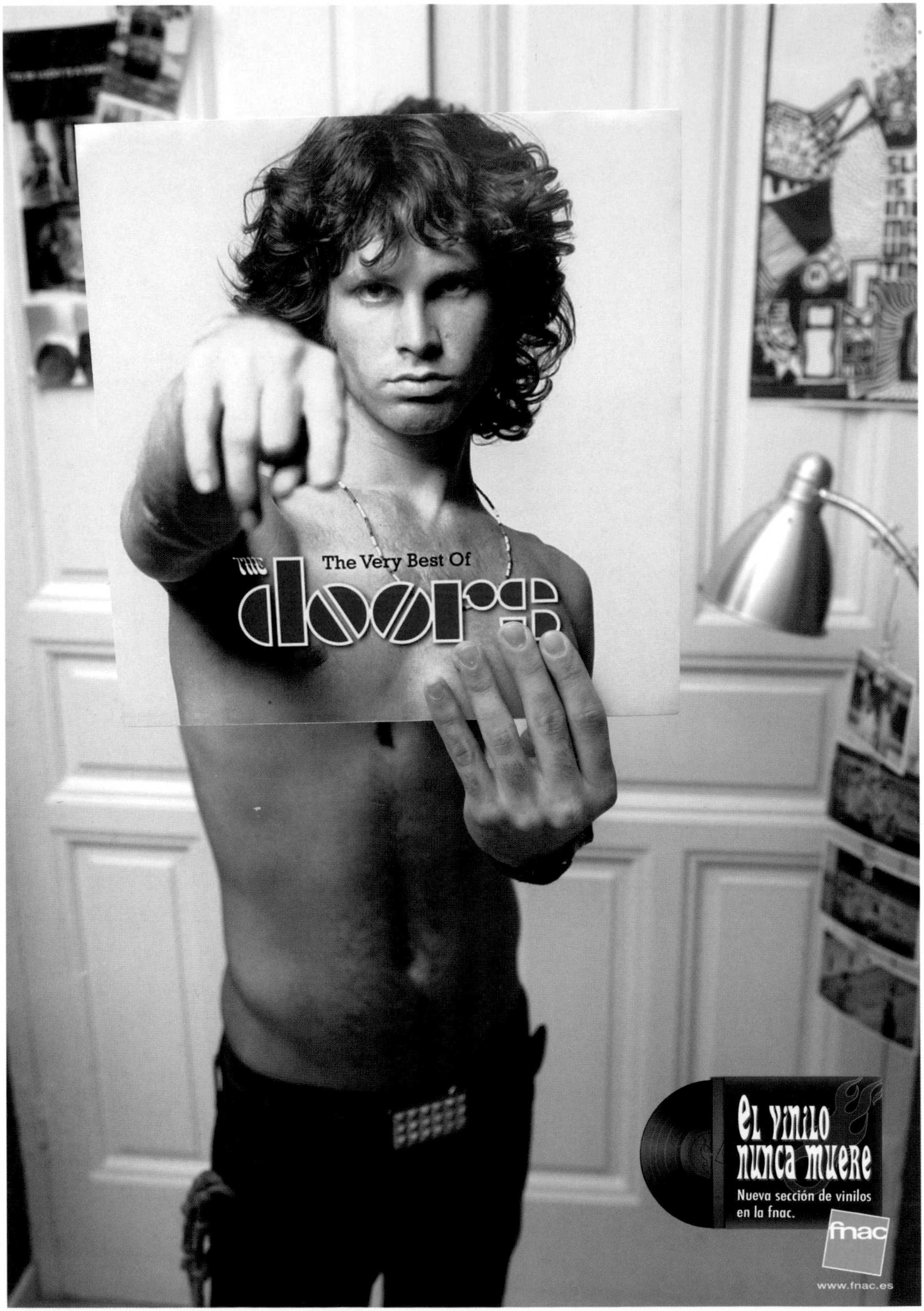

The Very Best Of
THE
doors

EL VINILO NUNCA MUERE
Nueva sección de vinilos en la fnac.
fnac
www.fnac.es

INTRO

STUNNING ADVERTISING, is a hard-hitting book on publicity. Remembering such as the Benetton campaigns some years ago, a company which opted for publicity without taboos in which we were presented with images opposing aids, hunger, and racism... we thought of doing this book. Selecting only those campaigns which provoked a sensation in the way we act. Those which leave us speechless, or those which bring out a smile, give us food for thought, the motivation to do something. Thanks to all the publicity agencies which have taken part and done their bit by handing over their images, expounding some of the most exceptional and credible campaigns in this project. What they have demonstrated is that behind each piece of advertising we see, whether on the streets, in the magazines, for sure publicity calls for some extraordinary work and great commitment to the consumer.

In the following pages we are going to see more than 400 printed ads created by different publicity agencies, highly regarded and well known the world over. A publicity campaign is comprised of a great many elements which have to be very carefully chosen to achieve the final result. That the advertised product captures the consumer's attention at the same time creating approval for this.

We also include a short biography of each agency and an explanation of one of the campaigns chosen to be featured in the book, as a way of having a better understanding of the motive behind the particular image or slogan chosen, etc., we will see how they go about directing their work at different publics, with different media and with the same objective, to create an IMPACT.

In spite of publicity being an enormously visual creative medium, the books dedicated to discovering a little more about this aspect of the media often turn out to be over descriptive and poorly illustrated.

We wanted principally to show their works, because we didn't want this to be a book aimed exclusively at the visual media sector, but also for all those of us interested by photography, graphic design, collage, publicity...

The publicity industry is undergoing a period of change. As a result, international companies are choosing to put more imaginative and original campaigns into practice with the aim of managing to speak of their products. This is the so-called "guerrilla publicity", which causes us to interact without knowing it, the campaigns being presented in an every day manner and adapted to our pace. (urban publicity).
Many agencies have leapt at this new formula and in this publication we include some of the leaders in the sector.

PUBLICIDAD DE IMPACTO, es un libro de publicidad impactante. Recordando campañas como las que realizó la empresa Benetton hace ya algunos años en los que apostaban por una publicidad sin tabúes con imágenes contra el sida, el hambre, el racismo... pensamos en realizar este libro. Recopilando sólo aquellas campañas que provocan alguna sensación en nuestra forma de actuar, aquellas que nos paralizan, nos sacan una sonrisa, nos hacen pensar, nos motivan a actuar.

Gracias a todas las agencias de publicidad que han participado y han puesto su granito de arena cediéndonos sus imágenes, explicándonos algunas de las campañas más destacadas y creyendo en este proyecto. Han demostrado que detrás de cada anuncio que podamos ver en revistas, vallas publicitarias, etc. hay un trabajo extraordinario y un gran compromiso con el consumidor.

En las siguientes páginas vamos a ver más de 400 anuncios impresos, dirigidos por distintas agencias de publicidad destacadas y conocidas en todo el mundo.
Una campaña publicitaria se compone de muchos elementos que han de estar muy bien escogidos para lograr un resultado final. Que el producto anunciado capte la atención del consumidor, creándole una aceptación por éste.

De cada agencia incluimos una breve biografía, y la explicación de una de las campañas seleccionadas para el libro, de esta forma podremos comprender mejor el motivo de la imagen, el eslogan escogido, etc., veremos como actúan dirigiendo sus trabajos a distintos públicos, con distintos medios y con un mismo objetivo IMPACTAR.

A pesar de que la publicidad es un medio creativo enormemente visual, los libros dedicados a descubrir un poco más este medio de comunicación, a menudo resultan demasiado descriptivos y poco ilustrados.
Nosotros queremos principalmente mostrar sus trabajos, porque no queremos que sea un libro exclusivamente dirigido al sector de la comunicación visual, si no a todos los que nos interesa la fotografía, el diseño gráfico, el collage, la publicidad...

La industria de la publicidad atraviesa un momento de cambio. Como resultado, las empresas internacionales están optando por poner en práctica campañas más imaginativas y originales con la finalidad de lograr que se hable de sus productos. Esta es la denominada "publicidad de guerrilla", la que nos hace interactuar sin nosotros saberlo, presentando las campañas de una forma cotidiana, adaptándolas a nuestro paso, (publicidad urbana).
Muchas agencias han dado el salto a esta nueva fórmula, en esta edición contamos con algunas de las más importantes en su sector.

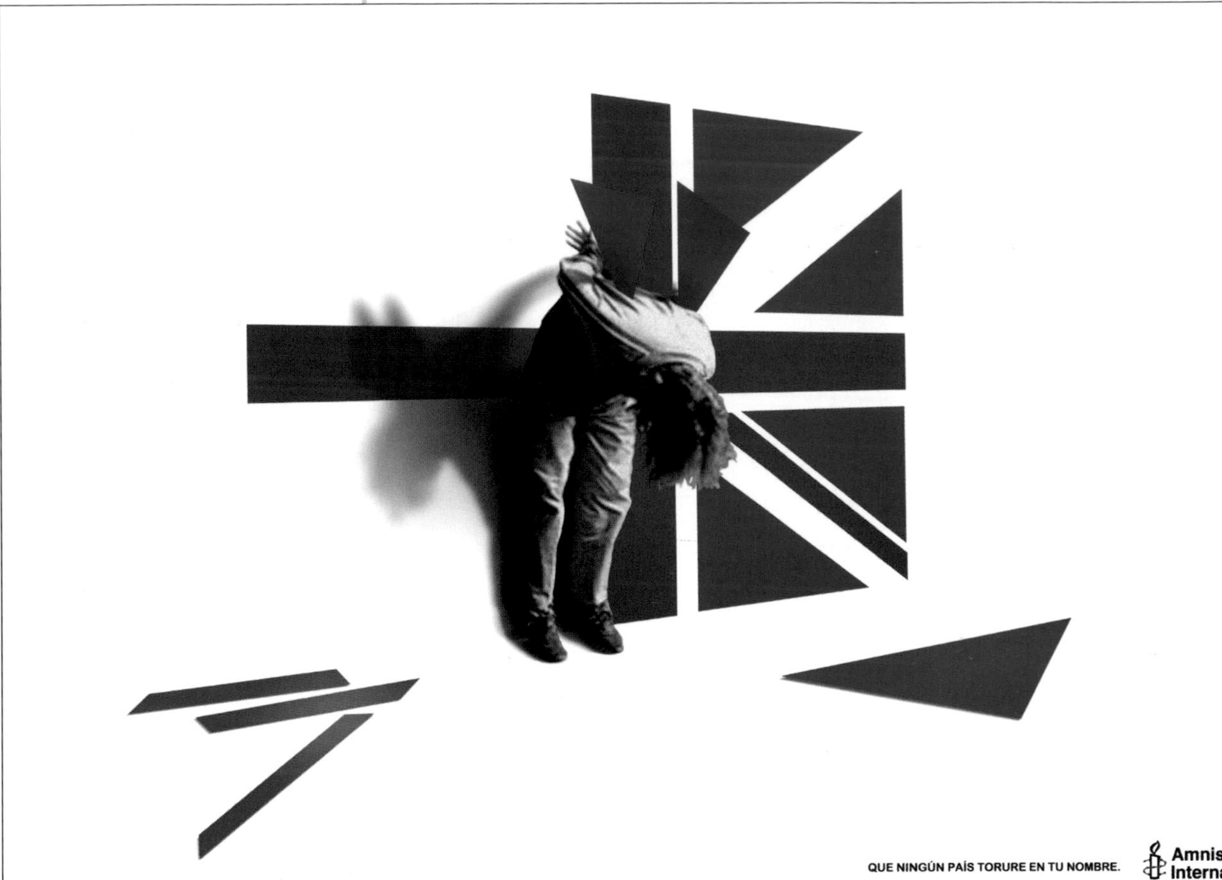
QUE NINGÚN PAÍS TORURE EN TU NOMBRE.
Amnistía Internacional

Antonio Montero
Creative Director at Contrapunto

However noisy it might be, firing a shot without taking aim means nothing. As an adolescent, every week I liked to see a page in the "10 minutos", magazine where they showed four images from international news agencies, at the foot of each were the words "To shout, to laugh, to cry and to run". And it was curious to see how every picture was matched to its corresponding caption. And I recall that I used to mentally swop these around with the images which very quickly came to signify something completely different and which I almost always liked a great deal more. Apart from the amusing aspect, the fact is I probably did it because I simply never agreed with the caption suggested for each image, in other words, I simply wasn't convinced. I don't know if this page is still in existence today but what it has taught me is that the famous thoughts of Unamuno "think what is felt, feel what is thought" are essential to understanding ourselves and our world and, certainly all those of us dedicated to communication in general, in the majority of cases have to combine a series of elements usually reduced to a picture with or without text or a text with or without a picture, etc., initially, to create an impact naturally and afterwards to transmit as much meaning and logic as possible with the unique and very important aim of achieving some extremely specific objectives. An impact yes, but with an aim, because to fire without taking aim....

Un disparo sin dirección no es nada por muy ruidoso que sea. Siendo aún adolescente, me encantaba ver cada semana una página en la revista "10 minutos" en la cual se mostraban cuatro imágenes de agencias de noticias internacionales y en las que se subtitulaba al pie de cada una de ellas. "Para gritar, para reír, para llorar y para correr". Y era curioso ver como casaba cada imagen con su correspondiente titular. Y recuerdo que solía cambiar mentalmente éstos con las imágenes y de pronto, se convertían y significaban otra cosa que casi siempre me gustaba mucho más. Aparte de divertirme, seguramente lo hacía porque simplemente no terminaba de estar de acuerdo con la propuesta de cada titular con su correspondiente imagen, es decir, no me habían convencido. No sé si aún hoy sigue existiendo esta página, pero lo que sí me demostró es que el famoso pensamiento de Unamuno "pensar lo sentido, sentir lo pensado" es fundamental para entendernos y entender nuestro mundo, ya que todos los que nos dedicamos a comunicar en general, tenemos que combinar en la mayoría de las ocasiones una serie de elementos que suelen reducirse a una imagen con texto o sin texto o un texto sin imagen, etc., para primero, impactar por supuesto y después transmitir todo el sentido y lógica posibles con el único e importantísimo fin de conseguir unos objetivos muy, muy concretos. Impactar sí, pero con sentido, porque un disparo sin dirección...

Eva Minguet Cámara
Publisher

I sincerely believe that the image is one of the most powerful forms of communication there is, despite the fact that without words I wouldn't be able to express myself, but I have always needed to see to believe.
We live in a world saturated with information, constantly being bombarded with more TV channels, new formulas to be happy, all types of music, magazines, films, web sites... never before has there been so many forms of distraction, we have become used to gather, store as use all this material.
How can we attract, with the minimum tools, the attention of a person swimming in a sea of stimuli?, I'm a strong supporter of the frozen image, of how it passes so easily through our retina to touch our heart, not without turning over in our minds, motivating us to act, to want, to help...
We don't need a voice on off to put us in the picture, nor music to put the good point, we are all capable of grasping the message by simply fixing our gaze, this is what we plan to show in this publication, so take a good look and enjoy the trip.

Creo sinceramente que la imagen es la forma de comunicación más poderosa que existe, y lo creo pese a que sin palabras no podría expresarme, pero siempre he necesitado ver para creer.
Vivimos en un mundo saturado de información, constantemente nos bombardean con más canales de televisión, nuevas fórmulas para ser felices, todo tipo de música, revistas, películas, paginas web... nunca antes se había tenido tantas formas de distracción, nos han acostumbrado a recopilar, almacenar y utilizar toda esta materia.
¿Cómo se puede captar, con las herramientas mínimas, la atención de una persona que nada en un mar de estímulos?, soy una defensora de la imagen congelada, de cómo puede traspasar nuestra retina, tocar nuestro corazón, no dejar de dar vueltas en nuestra mente, motivarnos a actuar, a desear, a ayudar...
No necesitamos una voz en off que nos narre la situación, ni una música que nos ponga el bello de punta, todos somos capaces de captar el mensaje con solo fijar nuestra mirada, esto es lo que mostraremos en esta edición, abran bien los ojos y disfruten del viaje.

Goodbye Innocence

"ME METÍ EN LA PRISIÓN DE LA ISLA DE SAINT JAMES PARA PODER TIRAR Y COGER JABONES EN LAS DUCHAS. CON ESTO ALCANCÉ UN FANTÁSTICO IMPULSO EN MI FAMOSO PASO DEL CANGURO."
KANGAROO STEP
1
2
3
4
5
6
UN AMERICANO ESTÁ DISPUESTO A TODO POR LLEGAR A SER UNA ESTRELLA DEL BAILE.
DANCELIFE, LUNES A LAS 21:00HS
MTV
MUSIC TELEVISION

TIEMPO bbdo

Campaing: Átomo Client: MTV España

Campaing: Canguro Client: MTV España

TIEMPO BBDO (Batten, Barton, Durstine & Osborn) began in New York in 1891 with a single employee. Now, 116 years on and this is the world's second ranking advertising agency with 20,500 employees, distributed over 77 different countries, 182 cities and 291 offices.

Omnicom came to be founded in 1986, one of the world's four biggest finance groups in the media.

Tiempo was an agency founded in Barcelona, Spain in 1960, which merged with BBDO in 1976, creating BBDO, with offices in Madrid and Barcelona.

TIEMPO BBDO (Batten, Barton, Durstine & Osborn) nació en Nueva York en 1891 con un único empleado. Hoy, 116 años después, es la segunda agencia de publicidad en el ranking mundial y posee 20.500 empleados, distribuidos en 77 países, 182 ciudades y 291 oficinas.

En 1986 nace Omnicom, uno de los cuatro grupos financieros de medios de comunicación más grandes del mundo.

En España, en 1960 se funda la agencia Tiempo en Barcelona, la cual se fusionaría con BBDO en el año 1976, creando Tiempo BBDO con oficinas en Madrid y Barcelona.

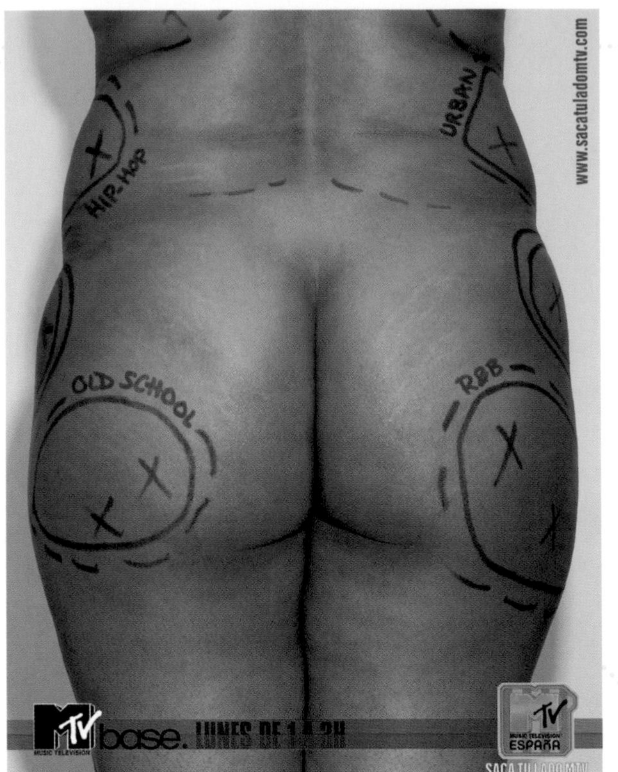

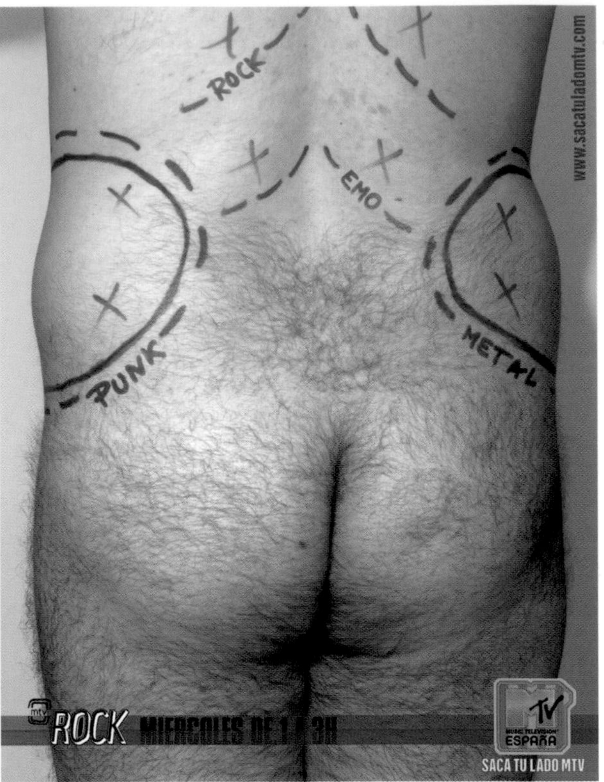

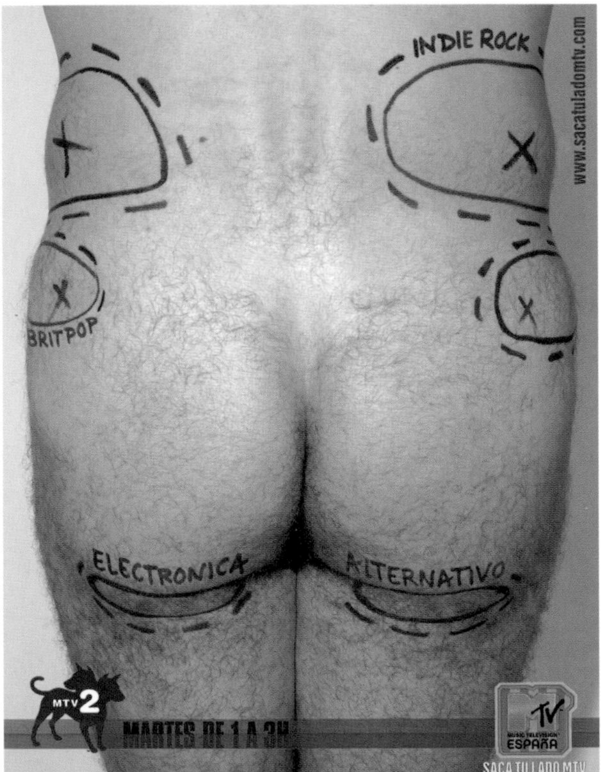

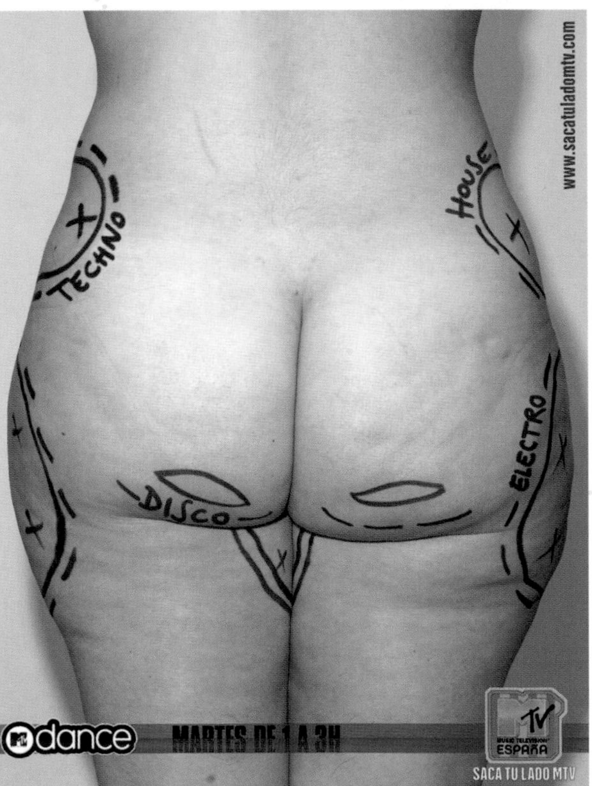

Campaing: Saca tu lado MTV Client: MTV España

Campaing: Pistón Client: MTV España

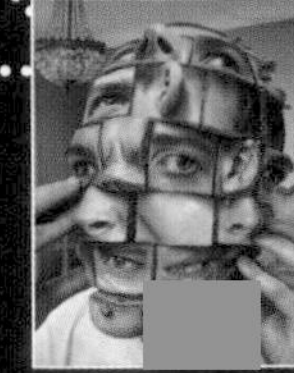

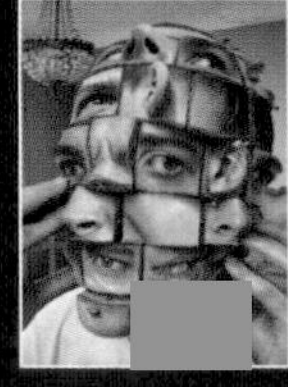

Campaing: Playstation 2 Client: Sony

Campaing: Playstation 2 Client: Sony

La Asociación Nuevo Renacer
presenta a los

HAPPINESS

Presentan su single: "Amo a Laura
pero esperaré hasta el matrimonio"

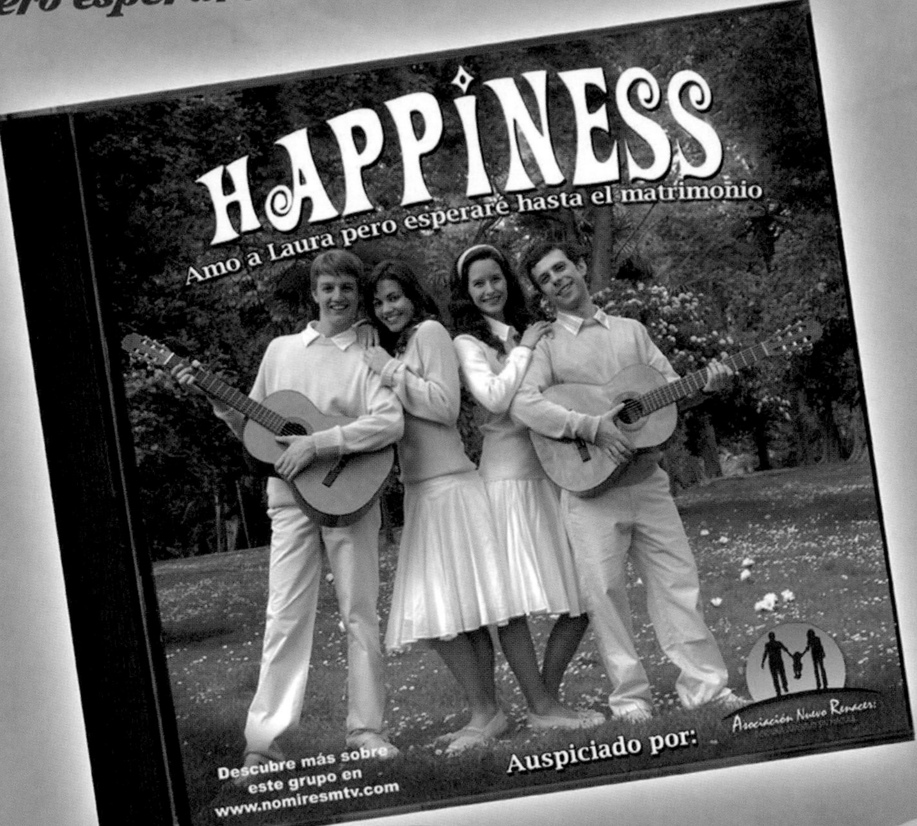

Por fin una alternativa a la poco
ejemplarizante música de la MTV

Más información en
www.nomiresmtv.com

Queremos una juventud con principios y valores sólidos, por eso nos revelamos ante los contenidos a menudo hirientes y poco ejemplarizantes de **MTV ESPAÑA.** Conoce más acerca de este movimiento en www.nomiresmtv.com

" MIS COMPAÑEROS QUEDAN PARA VER LA MTV, PERO YO SÉ DIVERTIRME SIN ENSUCIAR MI ESPÍRITU "
ENCUENTRA GENTE CON TUS MISMOS VALORES EN WWW.NOMIRESMTV.COM

¡¡JOVEN CON PRINCIPIOS, NO ESTÁS SOLO!!
Un montón de amigos te esperan lejos de la turbia influencia de MTV ESPAÑA.
Asociación Nuevo Renacer:
ENCUÉNTRALOS EN WWW.NOMIRESMTV.COM

Campaing: Amo a Laura Client: MTV España

The advertiser needed a communications plan of action to improve the fame of its brand (putting across the message the brand was local), to reach its target, to recover credibility as musical provider and improve its audience quota.

A note was added to their brief: "Due to the limited budget (60.000€), the proposed actions must have the effect of obtaining the best media coverage and create a media phenomenon".

Well...

The advertiser's audience increased by 50% in barely three weeks, becoming the leading channel amongst all the music stations and even reached 4th ranking amongst the most viewed theme channels. This brand's fame is extraordinary, within and outside its target, thanks to:

- 3.056.671 downloads of video clip "Amo a Laura".
- 2.349.418 visits to web page: www.nomiresmtv.com.
- 147.542 visits to web page: www.sacatuladomtv.com.
- 516.000 references appear in Google to "Amo a Laura" (120.000 speak of the advertiser).
- The "Amo a Laura" campaign has come to form part of the definition for Marketing Viral which appears in www.wikipedia.org.
- Internet users have approved of the campaign: there have been more than 80 different versions of the "Amo a Laura" video at www.youtube.com, they have made all different versions of the song, have created their own merchandising, have transformed the logo, created forums similar to our own and have even held theme parties in bars with "Amo a Laura" as the theme.

El anunciante necesitaba un plan de acciones de comunicación para mejorar la notoriedad de su marca (transmitiendo el mensaje de que su marca era local), acercarla a su target, recuperar la credibilidad como prescriptor musical y mejorar su cuota de audiencia.

Añadía una nota en su brief: "Debido al escaso presupuesto (60.000€), las acciones que se planteen deben buscar la provocación con el fin de obtener la mayor cobertura en medios y generar un fenómeno mediático".

Pues bien...

El anunciante aumentó su audiencia en casi un 50% en apenas tres semanas, convirtiéndose en el canal líder entre todas las cadenas de contenido musical, e incluso llegó a alcanzar el 4° puesto en el ranking de canales temáticos más vistos. La notoriedad de la marca es altísima, dentro y fuera de su target, gracias a:

- 3.056.671 descargas del videoclip de "Amo a Laura".
- 2.349.418 visitas a la página www.nomiresmtv.com.
- 147.542 visitas a la página www.sacatuladomtv.com.
- Aparecen 516.000 referencias en Google a "Amo a Laura" (120.000 hablan del anunciante).
- La campaña de "Amo a Laura" ha pasado a formar parte de la definición de Marketing Viral que aparece en www.wikipedia.org.
- Los usuarios de internet se han apropiado de la campaña: han subido más de 80 versiones diferentes del video de "Amo a Laura" a www.youtube.com, han hecho todo tipo de versiones de la canción, han creado su propio merchandising, han transformado el logo, se han creado foros paralelos al nuestro, e incluso han convocado fiestas temáticas en bares alrededor de "Amo a Laura".

NEW
eclipse

NEW!
eclipse
MIDNIGHT COOL

Campaing: Wringley Eclipse Client: Eclipse

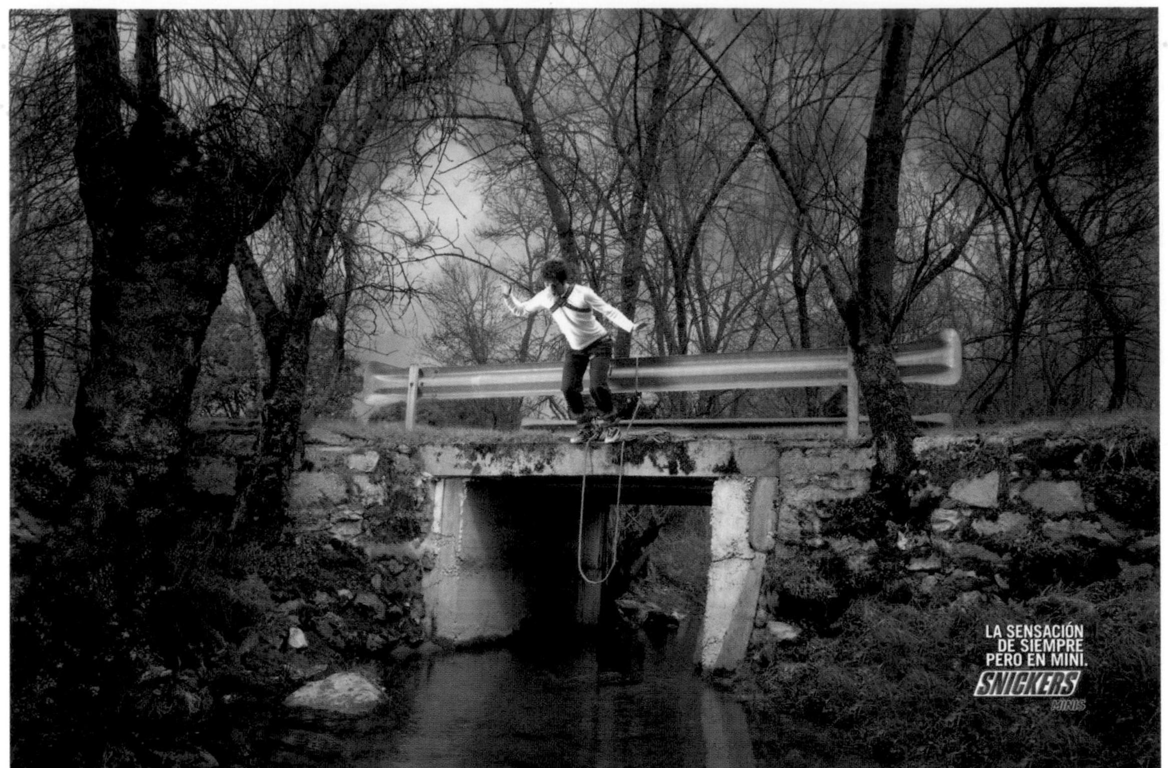

Campaing: Mini Extreme Client: Snickers

Campaing: Cooperativa Client: Cooperativa

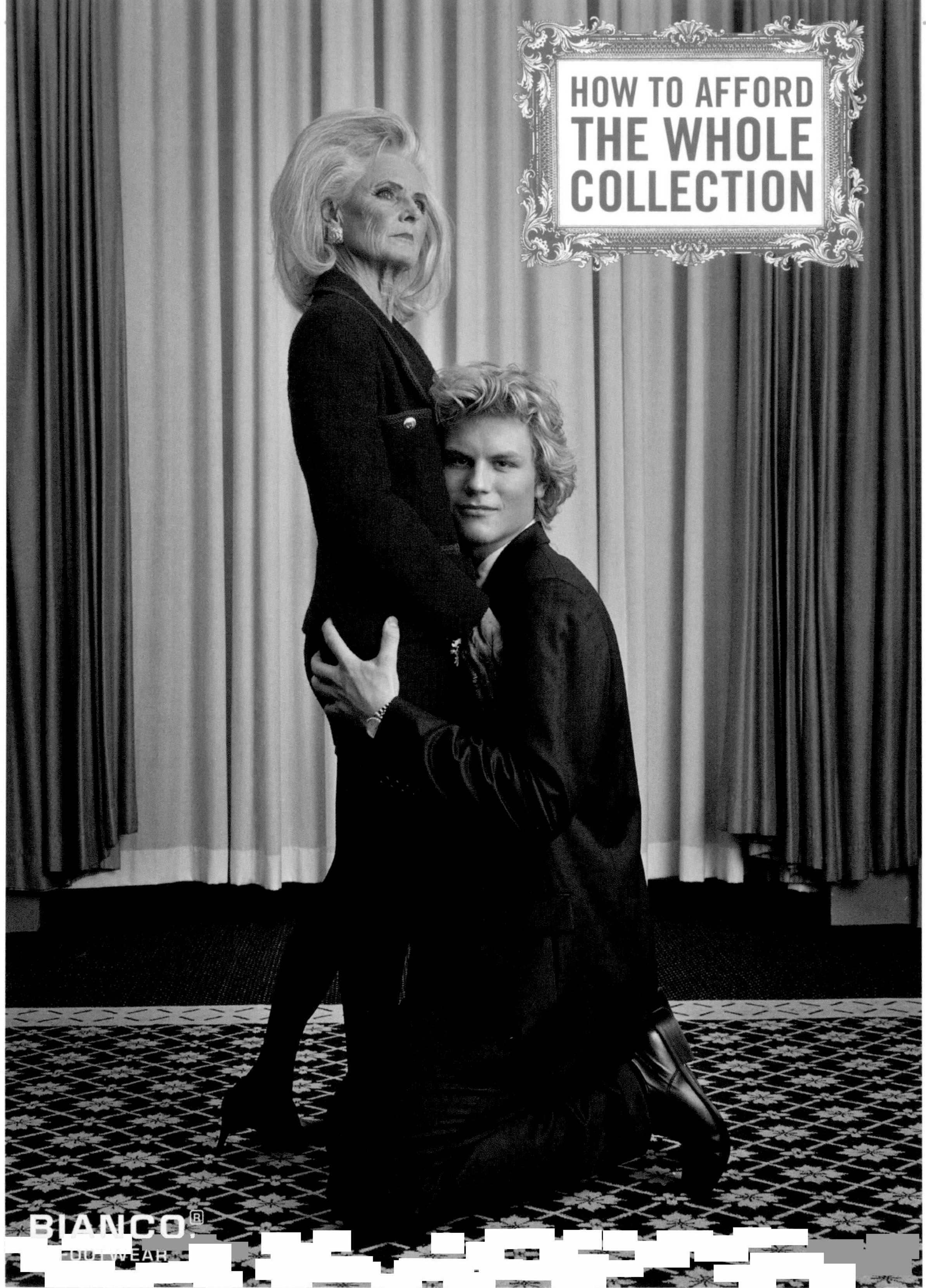
HOW TO AFFORD
THE WHOLE
COLLECTION
BIANCO®
FOOTWEAR

andco

HANDS ARE SO LAST YEAR
BIANCO.®
FOOTWEAR

Campaing: Hans are so last year Client: Bianco

Campaing: How to afford the whole collection Client: Bianco

The Agency employs 27 people with a high focus on creative advertising. We handle both international and local clients. All clients, who are focused on using communication and advertising as a tool to add value for their companies and brands. We work for Carlsberg, Audi, Seat and the largest Danish bank (Danske Bank) among others.

We have a strong belief that the power of strategy and creativity is a very strong asset for brands and advertisers if it is practiced properly. And we believe that strategy and creativity is equally important –and should be dealt with as one process and not as two independent. The result is often more and better creative work –and better results for clients. This process is not done alone by the agency. It is done in a very close collaboration with the client. Therefore our name & Co. We don't do work for our client –we do work with our client. When we work together with Carlsberg our name changes –to Carlsberg & Co, and when it is Audi it is Audi & Co.

La Agencia emplea a 27 personas y se especializa principalmente en publicidad creativa. Llevamos clientes internacionales y locales. Todos nuestros clientes utilizan la comunicación y la publicidad como herramienta para añadir valor a sus empresas y marcas. Trabajamos para Carlsberg, Audi, Seat y el mayor banco de Dinamarca (Danske Bank), entre otros.

Creemos firmemente que el poder de la estrategia y la creatividad es un gran recurso para marcas y anunciantes si se realiza adecuadamente. Y creemos que la estrategia y la creatividad son igualmente importantes, y deberían tratarse como un solo proceso y no como dos procesos independientes. Si se hace así, el resultado suele ser un trabajo mejor, más creativo y con mejores resultados para el cliente. Este proceso no solo lo lleva a cabo la agencia, sino que se realiza en estrecha colaboración con el cliente. De ahí nuestra denominación "nombre & Co". No trabajamos para nuestro cliente, sino que trabajamos con nuestro cliente. Cuando trabajamos con Carlsberg nuestro nombre cambia a Carlsberg & Co, y si se trata de Audi pasamos a ser Audi & Co.

Campaing: Transvestit Client: Bianco

Campaing: Designer Bags Client: Bianco

"& Co", has worked together with Bianco since the agency was founded –and in fact one of the creative directors, Thomas Hoffman has worked with Bianco for almost 16 years.

The strategy behind Bianco is to generate as much attention as possible in a young target group. To turn around the usual belief that small media budgets is an obstacle for creating result in communication. Bianco therefore tries to create maximum attention by being insightful, provocative surprising and daring. Attention to get PR on the advertising they do. On some campaigns Bianco har generated more than 10 times the value in PR that they have used on their advertising. A very effective tool to reach the youngsters, who constantly are searching for new fashion and shoes!

One example here is the "How to afford the whole collection" campaign. This campaign is based on the fact there are relationships between older men and younger women –known as "sugardaddy". This campaign makes fun of it, and explains that you can get the whole collection of these beautiful Bianco shoes if you have a sugardaddy –or sugarmom. There is also a version with an older woman and a younger man.

"& Co", ha trabajado con Bianco desde la fundación de la agencia y de hecho, uno de los directores creativos, Thomas Hoffman, trabajó con Bianco durante 16 años.

La estrategia que hay detrás de Bianco es generar la máxima atención posible en el grupo objetivo de los jóvenes, para cambiar la creencia popular de que los pequeños presupuestos mediáticos son un obstáculo para la creación de resultados en comunicación. Bianco escoge crear la máxima atención siendo intuitivo, provocativo, sorprendente y atrevido. Atención que sirva para obtener RP en la publicidad que hacen. En algunas campañas Bianco ha generado más de 10 veces el valor en RP de lo que han empleado en su publicidad. Se trata de una herramienta muy efectiva para llegar a los jóvenes, que buscan constantemente nuevas modas y zapatos.

Un buen ejemplo es la campaña "How to afford the whole collection", ("Cómo poder permitirse toda la colección"). Esta campaña se basa en las relaciones entre hombres mayores y mujeres más jóvenes, conocidos como "sugardaddy" (amante mayor y rico). Esta campaña se ríe de ello, y explica que puedes conseguir toda la colección de estos preciosos zapatos Bianco si tienes un amante viejo adinerado, o amante vieja adinerada, porque también hay una versión en la que aparece una mujer mayor con un chico joven.

HOW TO AFFORD
THE WHOLE
COLLECTION

BIANCO.®
FOOTWEAR

Campaing: How to afford the whole collection Client: Bianco

FALL
COLLECTION.03

BIANCO.®
FOOTWEAR

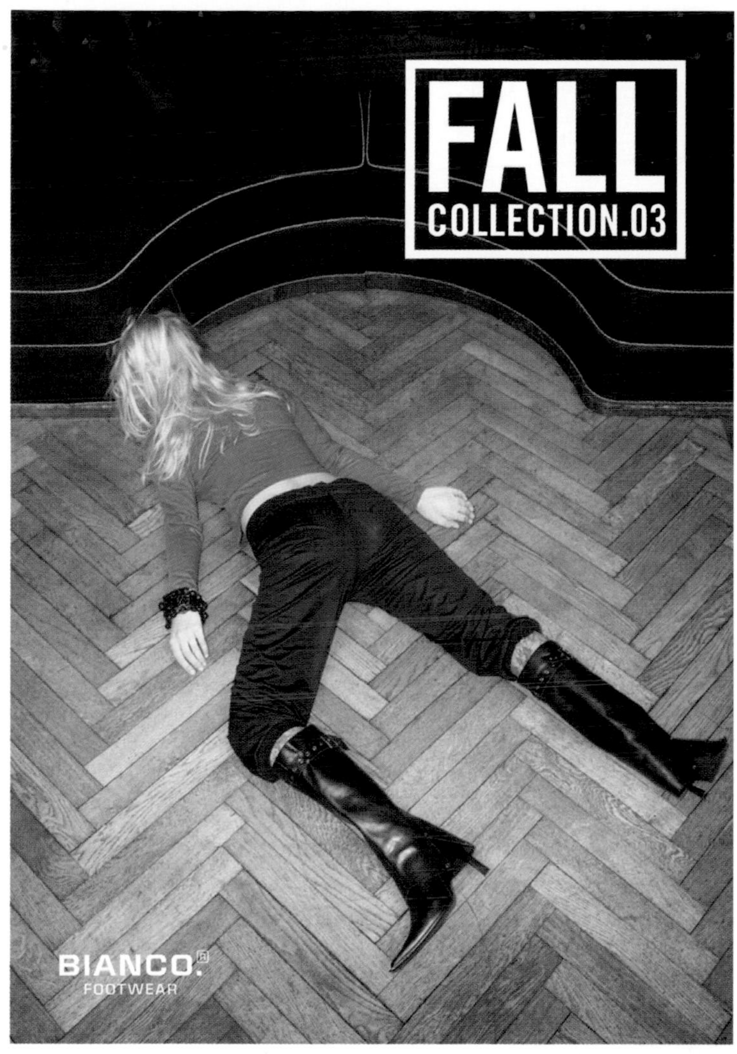

Campaing: Fall collection Client: Bianco

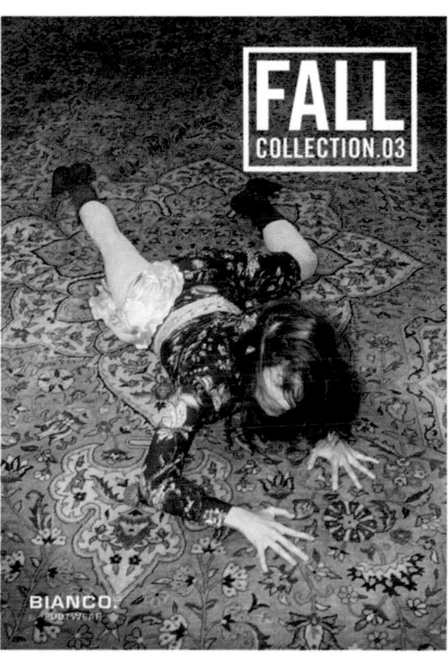

Campaing: The stiletto effect Client: Bianco

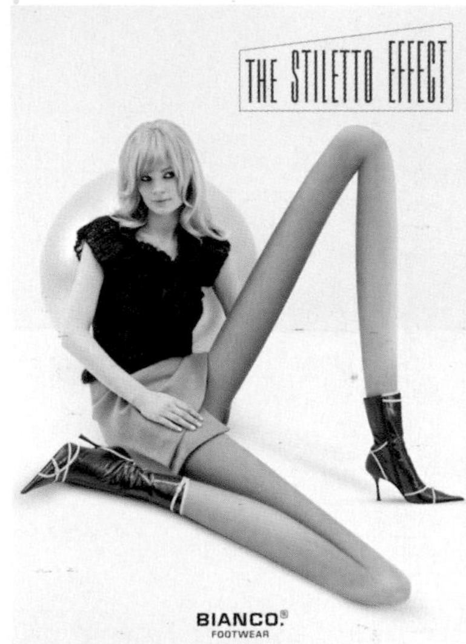

Campaing: Hans are so last year Client: Bianco

Campaing: Stay CHIC Client: Bianco

Men don't want to look at naked men
jbs
MENS UNDERWEAR

Men don't want to look at naked men
jbs
MENS UNDERWEAR

Campaing: Mens don't want to look at naked men Client: JBS

Campaing: **Sniff** Client: **JBS**

Campaing: **Devil inside** Client: **Bianco**

Campaing: Ichi Jeans Lauch Client: ICHI

United Colors of Benetton and Sisley are trademarks of Benetton Group SpA Italy Photo: O.Toscani

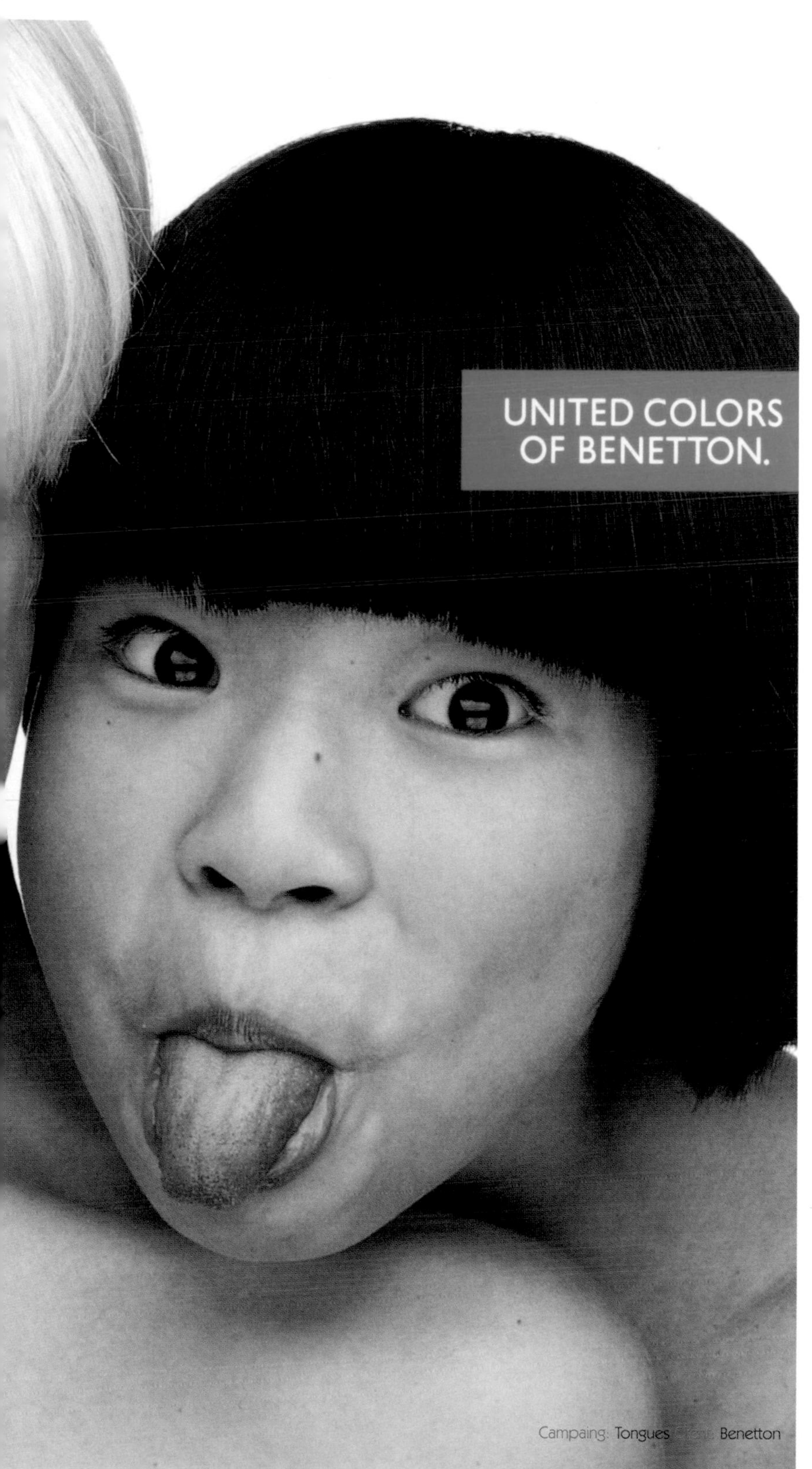

Campaing: Tongues Benetton

BENETTON

Benetton is present in 120 countries around the world with a strong italian character whose style, quality and passion are clearly seen in its brands: the casual United Colors of Benetton, fashion oriented Sisley and the leisurewear and streetwear brands Playlife and Killer Loop.

The Group has a total yearly production of around 150 million garments and a distribution network with 5,000 contemporary stores, mainly managed by independent partners, generating a total turnover of over 1,9 billion euro.

Established in 1965, Benetton is now controlled by Edizione Holding (a holding company wholly owned by the Benetton Family) with a 67% stake. It listed on the stock exchanges in Milan in 1986, in Frankfurt in 1988 and in New York in 1989.

Benetton está presente en 120 países de todo el mundo con un fuerte carácter italiano, cuyo estilo, calidad y pasión se ven reflejados en sus marcas: United Colors of Benetton es de estilo informal, Sisley está enfocada en la alta costura, las marcas Playlife y Killer Loop combina ropa deportiva y la ropa urbana.

El Grupo tiene una producción anual de unos 150 millones de prendas y una red de distribución con más de 5.000 tiendas contemporáneas, principalmente gestionadas por socios independientes, que generan una facturación total de más de 1,9 billones de euros.

Establecida en1965, Benetton está ahora bajo el control de Edizione Holding (una compañía tenedora propiedad de la Familia Benetton) con una participación del 67%.

Cotizó en bolsa en Milán en 1986, en Frankfurt en 1988 y en Nueva York en 1989.

Campaing: Albino Client: Benetton

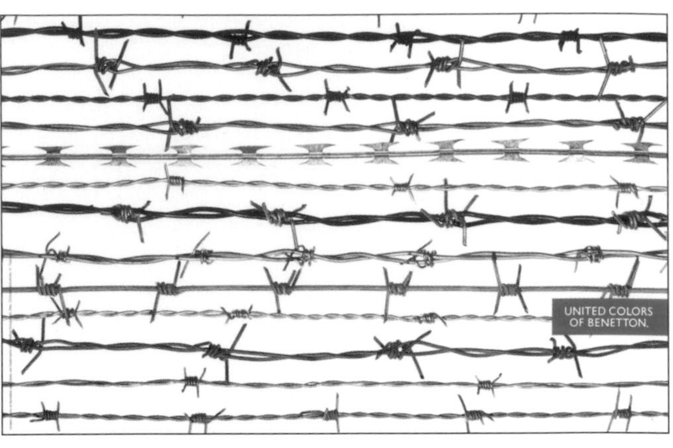

Campaing: Barbedwire Client: Benetton

Campaing: Bird Client: Benetton

Campaing: Handcuffs Client: Benetton

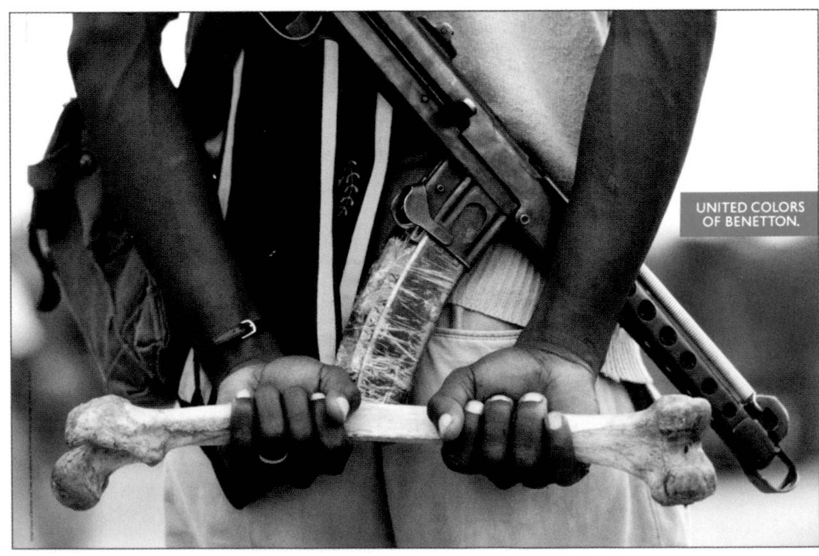

Campaing: Sodier with bone Client: Benetton

Campaing: Angel and evil Client: Benetton

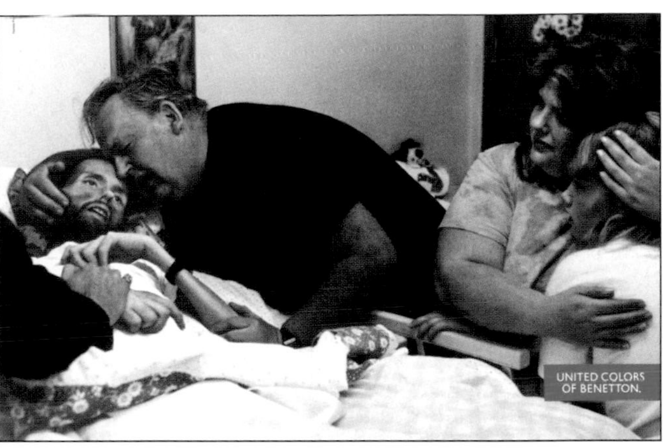

Campaing: AIDS David Kirby Client: Benetton

Campaing: Electric chair Client: Benetton

Campaing: Hearts Client: Benetton

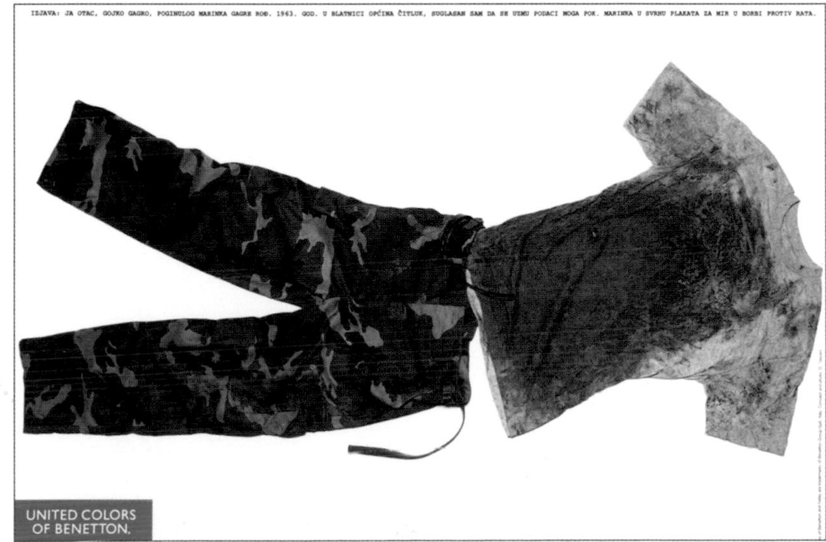

Campaing: Bosnia soldier Client: Benetton

Campaing: Food for work Client: Benetton

Campaing: Food for pace Client: Benetton

Campaing: Food to go home Client: Benetton

Campaing: Food for work Client: Benetton

Campaing: Food for life Client: Benetton

Ponzano, 13 February 2003. The global communication campaign for 2003, co-developed by United Colors of Benetton and the World Food Programme, the United Nations frontline agency in the fight against global hunger, re-establishes hunger as the world's most fundamental problem, since it is largely overlooked by both media and public opinion.

The images, taken by James Mollison, Fabrica's young photographer, in Afghanistan, Cambodia, Guinea and Sierra Leone, show crisis and poverty. They demonstrate how food becomes a catalyst for reconciliation and development, a tool capable of revolutionising the lives of hungry individuals.

Benetton is investing more than 15 million euro in over 30 countries for its 2003 campaign. This is part of a wider communication project on food, conceived and produced by Fabrica, including two other initiatives.

Colors 54 Food presents the dietary habits, the rites and time devoted to eating, drinking and preparing food in various parts of the world (with a supplement developing the 2003 United Colors of Benetton campaign). Food –as a means of communication, artistic expression and design –is the subject of a book entitled 2,398 gr (the actual weight of the book itself) produced by Fabrica and published by Electa. Young artists from the Benetton centre, together with others of international acclaim, were invited to represent food, each in their own personal way –as a fetish, ritual, excess, dependence, celebration, emotion, reflection, contradiction, oppression and obsession.

Ponzano, 13 Febrero de 2003. La campaña de comunicación global para 2003, codesarrollada por United Colors of Benetton y el Programa Mundial de Alimentos, la agencia de las Naciones Unidas que lucha contra el hambre, vuelva a situar el hambre como el principal problema del mundo, puesto que se trata de un tema que tanto los medios como la opinión pública han pasado por alto.

Las imágenes tomadas por el joven fotógrafo de Fabrica James Mollison en Afganistán, Camboya, Guinea y Sierra Leona, muestran la crisis y la pobreza. Demuestran que la comida es un factor decisivo para la reconciliación y el desarrollo, una herramienta capaz de revolucionar la vida de los individuos hambrientos.

Benetton invirtió más de 15 millones de euros en más de 30 países para su campaña de 2003. La campaña forma parte de un proyecto de comunicación más extenso dedicado a la comida ideado y producido por Fabrica, que comprende también otras dos iniciativas.

Colors 54 Food presenta los hábitos alimentarios, los ritos y el tiempo dedicados a comer, beber y preparar comida en varias partes del mundo (con un suplemento que amplía la campaña de United Colors of Benetton de 2003). La comida como medio de comunicación, expresión artística y diseño, es el tema de un libro titulado 2.398 gr. (el peso del libro) producido por Fabrica y editado por Electa. Jóvenes artistas del centro Benetton, junto con otros artistas de renombre internacional, fueron invitados a representar la comida a su manera: como fetiche, ritual, exceso, dependencia, celebración, emoción, reflexión, contradicción, opresión y obsesión.

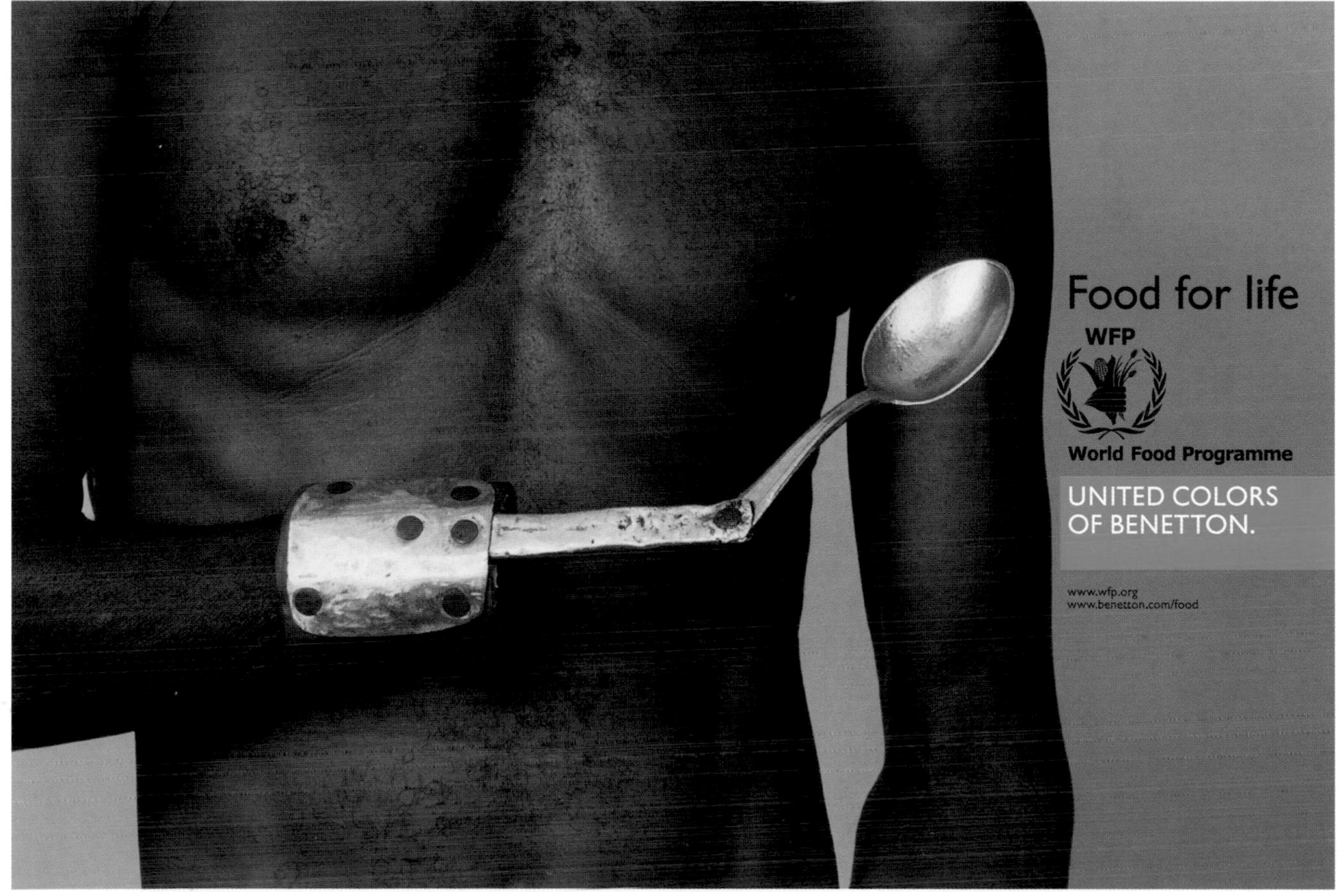

UNITED COLORS
OF BENETTON.

Campaing: Priest and Nun Client: Benetton

Campaing: 40th anniversary Client: Benetton

Campaing: Human rigts Client: Benetton

Campaing: Breastfeeding Client: Benetton

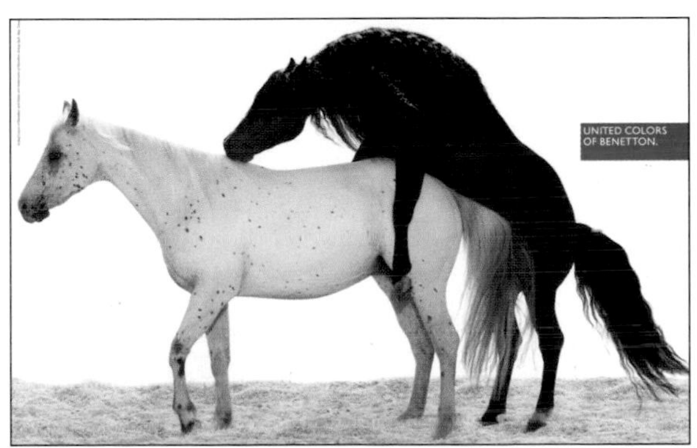

Campaing: Horses Client: Benetton

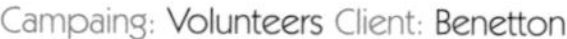
Campaing: Volunteers Client: Benetton

Campaing: Volunteers Client: Benetton

Berlin, 25th September 2001. A former member of a street gang, who still bears the signs of his past life tattooed on his skin, now fights against violence, a young lawyer promotes and defends human rights, a transvestite distributes condoms amongst prostitutes; an elderly tap dancer entertains residents in old people's homes. They come from every nation around the world, they have diverse backgrounds, they are young or not-so-young but they have in common the same feeling of commitment to the weak and suffering. They are the endorsers for United Colors of Benetton's communication campaign for autumn 2001 produced in collaboration with United Nations volunteers (the United Nations' programme that has been dealing with voluntary action around the world for the past thirty years) for the International Year of Volunteers, whose celebrations will culminate on 5th December 2001 with International Volunteer Day.
In this new press and billboard campaign, photographed by James Mollison, one of the young creative talents of Fabrica, Benetton deals with a subject that is typical of its communication strategy, and once again, talks about "real people", touching on important issues for a civilised society.
During the campaign's conception stage Fabrica (Benetton's Communication Research Centre) studied various ways of being a volunteer in today's world, focusing on the more unusual aspects and showing that devoting one's time and energy to others also leads the way to self-improvement and to achieving a better quality of life.

Berlín, 25 de septiembre de 2001. Un antiguo miembro de una banda callejera, que todavía luce tatuados en la piel los símbolos de su vida pasada, lucha ahora contra la violencia, un joven abogado promueve y defiende los derechos humanos, un travestido distribuye preservativos entre las prostitutas, una vieja bailarina de claqué anima a los ancianos internados en residencias. Provienen de distintas naciones del mundo, han vivido las experiencias más diversas, son jóvenes y no tan jóvenes, pero todos ellos comparten el mismo sentimiento de compromiso hacia los débiles y los que sufren. Son los testimonios de la campaña de comunicación de United Colors of Benetton para el otoño 2001, realizada en colaboración con voluntarios de las Naciones Unidas (el programa de las Naciones Unidas que desde hace treinta años se ocupa del voluntariado en el mundo), con ocasión del Año Internacional de los Voluntarios, cuyas celebraciones culminarán el 5 de diciembre de 2001 en el día dedicado a los voluntarios de todos los países.
Con esta nueva campaña internacional en prensa y vallas. Fotografiada por uno de los creativos de Fabrica, James Mollison, Benetton trata uno de los temas típicos de su comunicación, que una vez más habla de "gente de verdad" y toca problemas concretos de la vida de la sociedad.
Al idear la campaña, Fabrica (el Centro de Investigación sobre la comunicación de Benetton) ha indagado sobre los distintos modos de ser voluntario hoy en día, destacando los aspectos más insólitos y mostrando que también podemos dedicarle nuestro tiempo y nuestros esfuerzos a los demás para mejorar nosotros mismos y nuestra propia calidad de vida.

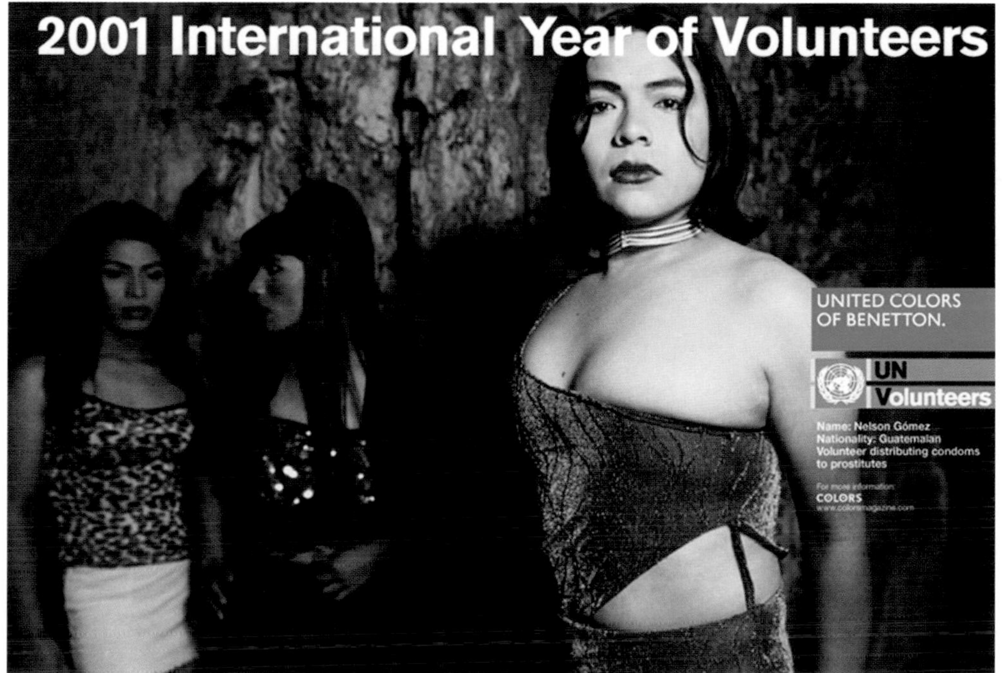

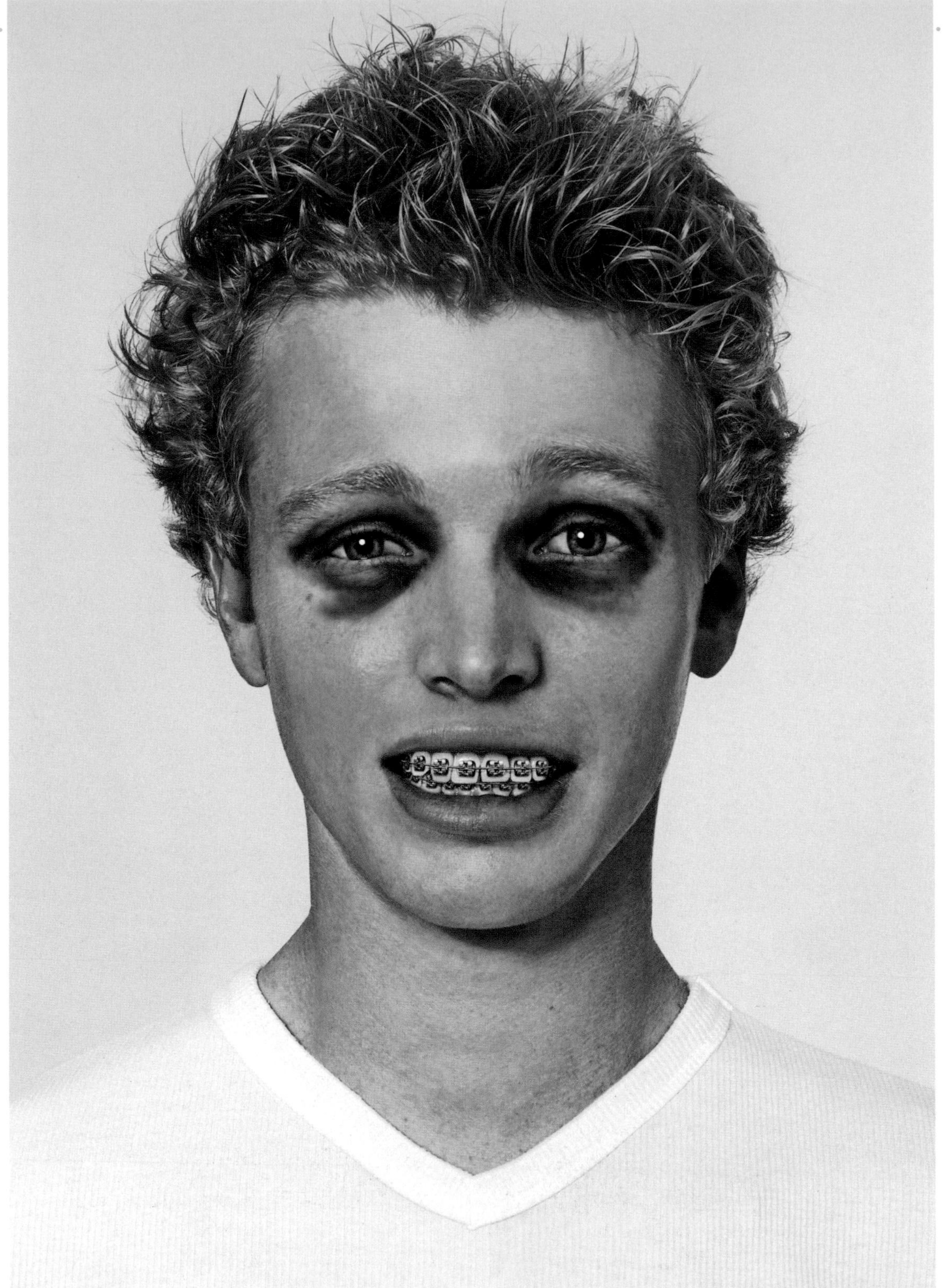
Now with a Magnetic Clasp.
THE ONE AND ONLY
Wonderbra

foxp2

Heading up the FOXP2 lab are Andrew Whitehouse, Noel Cottrell, Justin Gomes, and Charl Thom.

FOXP2 is the scientific name give to the creativity and communication gene that has mutated in humans over the last 50.000 years.

"THE FREEDOOM TO MUTATE"

FOXP2 is a dynamic, hands-on agency with the local and international experience, ability and people to mutate to find the most creative and effective solution to any marketing challenge.

La agencia FOXP2 está dirigida por Andrew Whitehouse, Noel Cottrell, Justin Gomes y Charl Thom.

FOXP2 es el nombre científico del gen de la creatividad y la comunicación que ha mutado en los humanos a lo largo de los últimos 50.000 años.

"THE FREEDOOM TO MUTATE"

FOXP2 es una agencia dinámica y práctica con la experiencia local e internacional, la habilidad y el personal necesarios para mutar con el objetivo de encontrar la solución más creativa y efectiva a cualquier reto de marketing.

Campaing: Kids magazine Client: National Geographic

Campaing: Now with a magnetic claps Client: Wonderbra

Old Khaki
SA HOMEGROWN

They don't have to learn the hard way.

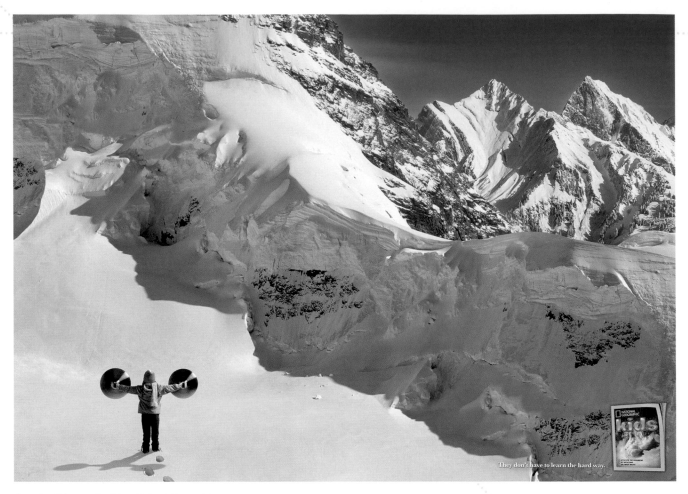

Campaing: Kids magazine Client: National Geographic

Campaing: Kids magazine Client: National Geographic

POLICE

Old Khaki
SA HOMEGROWN

Old Khaki
SA HOMEGROWN

Campaing: Sa romegrown Client: Old Khaki

>> No more parking space problems.
smart
open your mind.
pace problems.
open

JVM

Campaing: Tear-off parking lots Client: DaimlerChrysler SMART

Background Jung Von Matt/Limmat.

The communication agency Jung Von Matt/Limmat was established in 1993 in Zurich and has a team of 70 working in the areas of advertising, PR, web media and dialog. The latest Media Research Group survey conducted among Switzerland's 500 biggest advertising clients ranks Jung Von Matt/Limmat first in terms of image, name recognition, and recommendation rate. The agency's client base includes Julius Baer, Health Promotion Switzerland, Canton Graubünden, the HandelsZeitung business newspaper, Hug, Interpharma/Vips, Jura, Max Shoes, Mercedes-Benz, Migros Bank, Mövenpick Hotels & Resorts, the Saisonküche culinary magazine, SI Style, Vespa, Panasonic, Rivella International, SBB, Smart, Swisscom and Ramseier.

Origen de Jung Von Matt/Limmat.

La agencia de comunicación Jung Von Matt/Limmat fue fundada en 1993 en Zurich y cuenta con un equipo de 70 personas que trabajan en los ámbitos de la publicidad, RP, medios y diálogos Web. La última encuesta de Media Research Group realizada entre los 500 mayores clientes de publicidad de Suiza sitúa en primer lugar a Jung Von Matt/Limmat en términos de imagen, reconocimiento del nombre e índice de recomendación. La base de clientes de la agencia incluye a Julius Baer, Health Promotion Switzerland, Canton Graubünden, el periódico económico HandelsZeitung, Hug, Interpharma/Vips, Jura, Max Shoes, Mercedes-Benz, Migros Bank, Mövenpick Hotels & Resorts, la revista de cocina Saisonküche, SI Style, Vespa, Panasonic, Rivella International, SBB, Smart, Swisscom y Ramseier.

MINI INSTALLATION.

VIEW FROM ROOFTOP.

THE BASE JUMP FOR MINI.

THE CHALLENGE.
In 2006 the MINI was re-launched. Its key feature: more power for an even more sporty driving experience. The re-launch's motto was "Incredibly MINI. The new MINI." And when MINI says "incredible", they mean incredible.

THE SOLUTION.
As incredible as jump
another. And this not
used road of Zurich, v
No sooner thought th
and placed a new MI
campaign slogan "Inc
large tarpaulin.

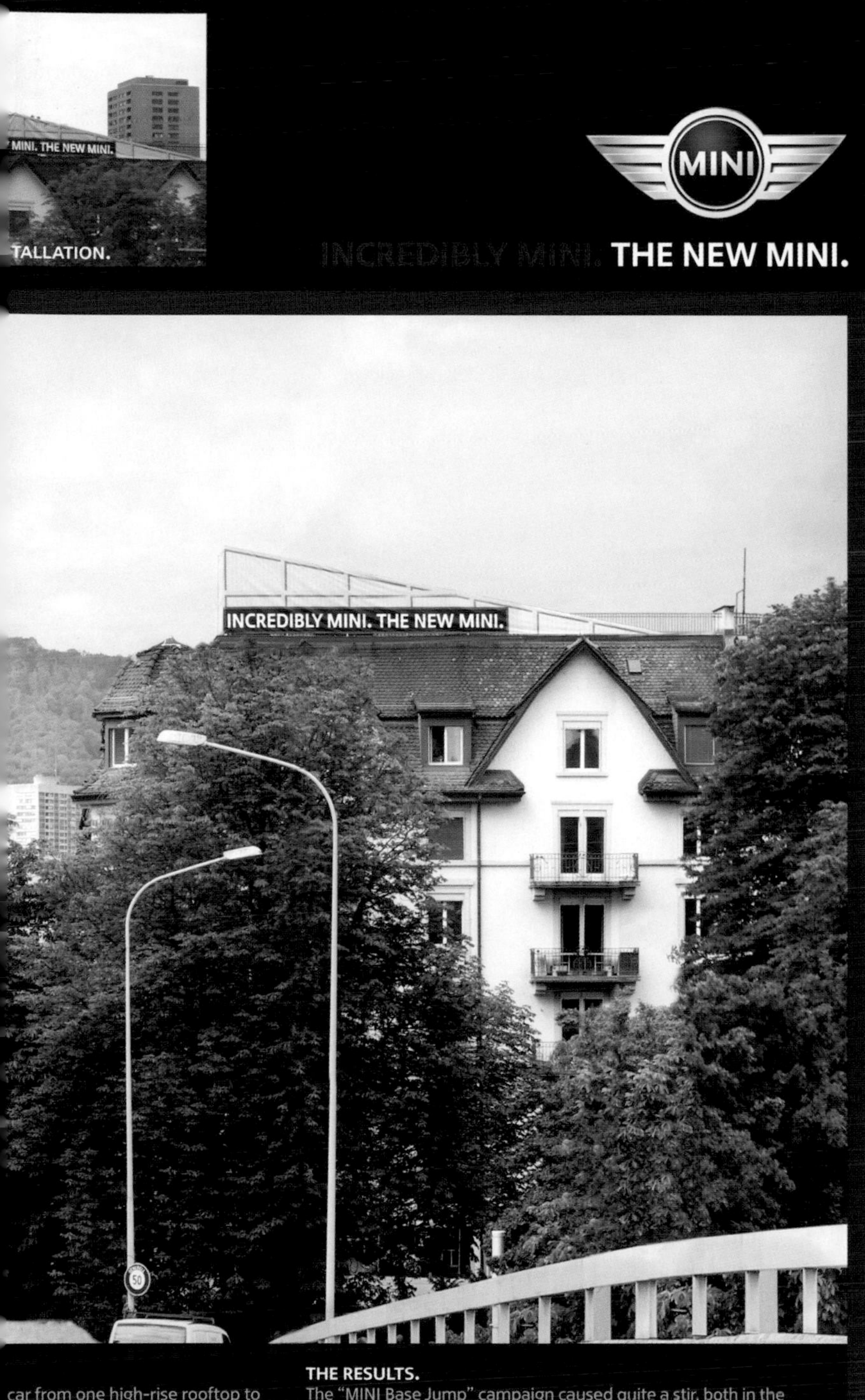

MINI. THE NEW MINI.
TALLATION.
MINI
THE NEW MINI.
INCREDIBLY MINI. THE NEW MINI.
50
car from one high-rise rooftop to
here, but close to the most heavily
80,000 cars driving by every day.
Ve installed a ramp on one rooftop,
on the one next to it – with the
NI. The new MINI," printed on a
THE RESULTS.
The "MINI Base Jump" campaign caused quite a stir, both in the
media ("Are they allowed to do this?") and among the over 80,000
drivers ("Is this possible?") crossing the nearby bridge every day.
The campaign's goal was to invite people to go for a test drive
at their nearest MINI dealership – because statistics show that 60 %
of those who try one, buy one.

Campaing: Base Jump Client: BMW MINI

Thanks to its range of even more powerful engines, the new MINI is more confident than ever –which pushes the nimble car to the most incredible of driving stunts. It's fiery temperament was demonstrated by an installation placed on the rooftop of a prominent Zurich twin high-rise, a location visible from all corners, right next to the busiest street of the city. On one of the buildings, a ramp was put up, and on the other, a real-size model of the new MINI –creating the illusion that the compact car had really just made that giant leap.

Gracias a su nueva gama de motores todavía más potentes, el nuevo MINI es más seguro que nunca lo cual permite que el hábil coche pueda realizar las acrobacias más increíbles. Su temperamento ardiente se demostró por medio de una instalación colocada en la azotea de dos rascacielos gemelos de Zurich, una ubicación visible desde todos los rincones, justo al lado de la calle más concurrida de la ciudad. En uno de los edificios se colocó una rampa, y en el otro, un modelo a tamaño real del nuevo MINI, creando la ilusión de que el compacto coche acaba de hacer el enorme salto.

Campaing: Sushi hay-rolls Client: Yooji's

In Switzerland hay is pressed into rolls and wrapped in white foil. These white rolls are stacked in front of farms, on pastures or at roadsides.
For our ambient media advertising we selected these stacks at the roadside. In the middle of each hay-roll in the stack we pasted a sticker showing the inner part of a sushi roll.
The result: the hay-rolls looked like giant sushi-california-rolls, thus perfectly promoting our client Yooji's, one of Zurich's top Sushi-Restaurants.

En Suiza, el heno se prensa en rollos y se embala con papel blanco. Estos rollos blancos se amontonan delante de granjas, pastos o en los bordes de carreteras.
Para nuestra publicidad "Ambient Media", (publicidad en soporte exterior), seleccionamos estos montones en los bordes de las carreteras. En medio de cada uno de los rollos de heno pegamos una pegatina que muestra la parte interior de un rollo de sushi.
El resultado: los rollos de heno parecen "rollos de sushi california" gigantes, con lo cual promocionamos el restaurante Yooji de nuestro cliente, uno de los mejores restaurantes de sushi de Zurich.

Campaing: Tear-off parking lots Client: DaimlerChrysler SMART

With a wheelbase of only 180 cm, the smart is one of the smallest cars in the world, barely taking up the space of a standard F200 poster.
For our campaign, we produced over-sized poster pads containing a number of "parking lots", ready for tear-off. Just like their smaller counterparts, they had perforated pages, with each pad containing a total of 20 parking lots. The tear-off posters were installed at strategic inner city locations –particularly in those places where parking lots are truly hard to come by.

Con una distancia entre ejes de solo 180 cm., el smart es uno de los coches más pequeños del mundo, que apenas ocupa el espacio de un póster F200 estándar.
Para nuestra campaña, creamos unos bloques de posters descomunales, que contienen un número de "aparcamiento" listos para arrancar. Igual que sus homólogos más pequeños, tenían páginas perforadas y cada bloque contenía un total de 20 aparcamientos.
Los pósteres arrancables se instalaron en lugares estratégicos del centro de la ciudad, especialmente en lugares donde es prácticamente imposible encontrar aparcamiento.

Que
tu oído
no te
aleje
MicroAudio
CENTROS AUDITIVOS

KITCHEN

The publicity agency by the name of Kitchen is an agency apart. For this reason it goes by the name of: The publicity agency by the name of Kitchen.
This is a blank agency, very blank on the walls and in spirit, so much so that the good thing which comes out of its campaigns has become this agency's main form of identity.
This also happens to be an agency which has gained considerable weight during its 6 year existence, amongst other things on account of the increase in the number of professionals: more than 30 active thinking minds at the service of creativity, design, strategic planning or keeping the books. An above all, at the service of advertisers such as Kia, Cuatro, ONO, MultiOpticas, Fnac, Mutua Madrileña Masters Madrid and ICEX - Wines from Spain (International promoter of Spanish wines).
Not forgetting the increased weight has also made an impact premier wise at Spanish festivals and others beyond the frontier (FIAP, New York Festivals, Laus and CdC).
In the end, gaining weight was something only to be expected in a publicity agency by the name of Kitchen, as opposed to Bathroom.

La agencia de publicidad que tiene por nombre Kitchen es una agencia independiente. Por algo se llama así: La agencia de publicidad que tiene por nombre Kitchen.
Es una agencia blanca, muy blanca de paredes y de espíritu, tanto que el buen rollo que respiran sus campañas se ha convertido en su principal seña de identidad.
También es una agencia que ha engordado bastante en sus 6 años de existencia, entre otras cosas por el incremento del número de profesionales: más de 30 mentes pensantes puestas al servicio de la creatividad, el diseño, la planificación estratégica o la labor de cuentas. Y sobre todo, puestas al servicio de anunciantes como Kia, Cuatro, ONO, MultiOpticas, Fnac, Mutua Madrileña Masters Madrid o ICEX - Wines from Spain (promoción de los vinos de España a nivel internacional).
Sin olvidar que en el aumento de peso también ha influido algún que otro premio que ha tocado en festivales españoles y de más allá de la frontera (FIAP, New York Festivals, Laus o CdC).
Y es que, al final, engordar era algo previsible en una agencia de publicidad que tiene por nombre Kitchen. Y no Bathroom.

Que tu oído no te aleje
MICROAUDIO

Campaing: Que tu oído no te aleje Client: Multiópticas

Toda la música, en Fnac Donostia

Abrimos el miércoles 21 de septiembre
en el Mercado San Martin

La mayor oferta de Donostia en música, informática, imagen y sonido, cine y libros al precio mínimo garantizado

www.fnac.es

Todo el cine, en Fnac Donostia

Abrimos el miércoles 21 de septiembre
en el Mercado San Martin

La mayor oferta de Donostia en cine, informática, imagen y sonido, libros y música al precio mínimo garantizado

www.fnac.es

Campaing: Apertura Fnac Donostia Client: Fnac

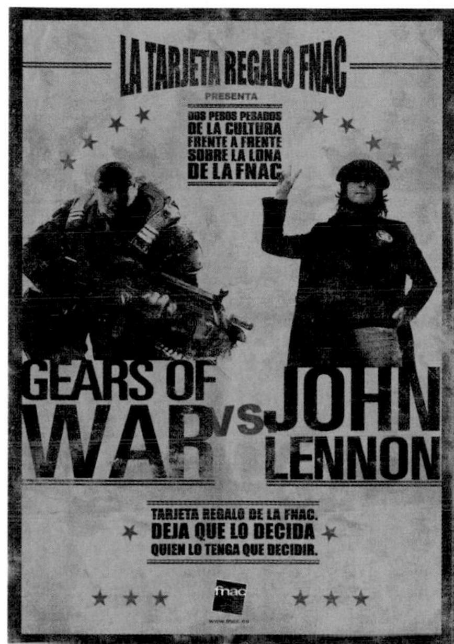

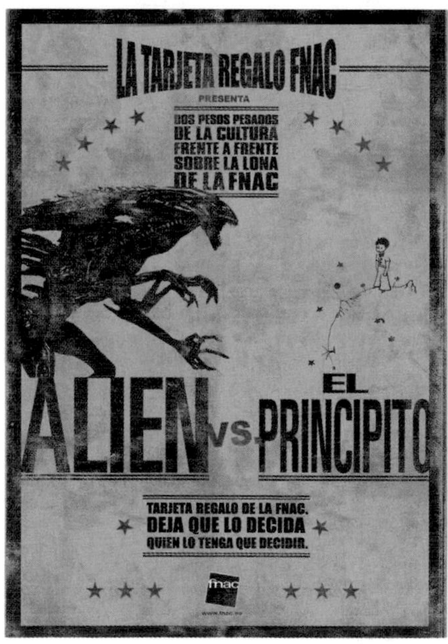

LA TARJETA REGALO FNAC
PRESENTA
DOS PESOS PESADOS
DE LA CULTURA
FRENTE A FRENTE
SOBRE LA LONA
DE LA FNAC
GEARS OF WAR
VS.
JOHN LENNON
TARJETA REGALO DE LA FNAC.
DEJA QUE LO DECIDA
QUIEN LO TENGA QUE DECIDIR.
fnac

LA TARJETA REGALO FNAC
PRESENTA
DOS PESOS PESADOS
DE LA CULTURA
FRENTE A FRENTE
SOBRE LA LONA
DE LA FNAC
ALIEN
VS.
EL PRINCIPITO
TARJETA REGALO DE LA FNAC.
DEJA QUE LO DECIDA
QUIEN LO TENGA QUE DECIDIR.
fnac

LA TARJETA REGALO FNAC
PRESENTA
DOS PESOS PESADOS
DE LA CULTURA
FRENTE A FRENTE
SOBRE LA LONA
DE LA FNAC
EL EXORCISTA
VS.
ALICE COOPER
TARJETA REGALO DE LA FNAC.
DEJA QUE LO DECIDA
QUIEN LO TENGA QUE DECIDIR.
fnac
www.fnac.es

Campaing: Tarjeta regalo Client: Fnac

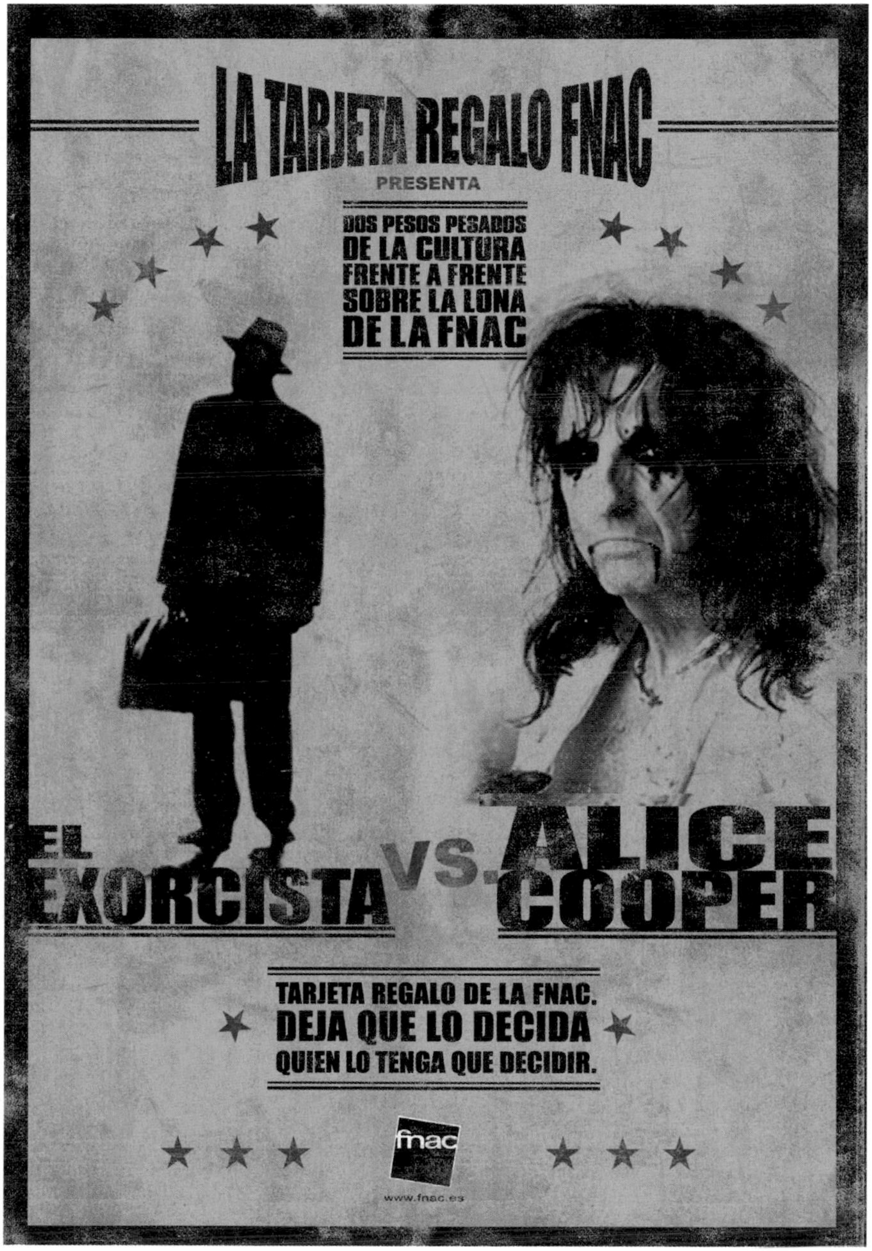

El vinilo nunca muere

Nueva sección de vinilos en la fnac.

fnac

www.fnac.es

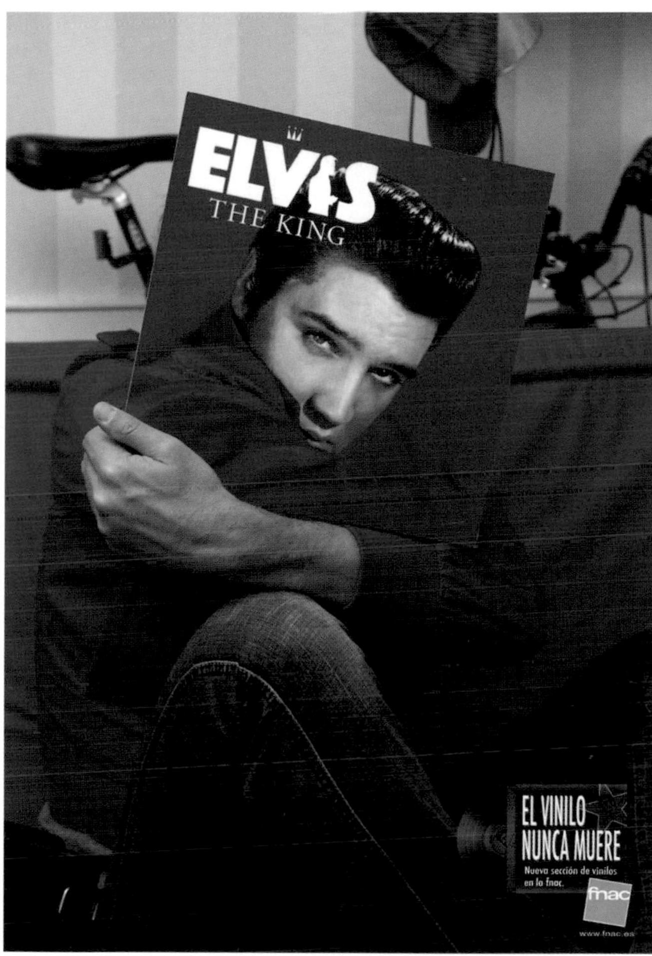

Campaing: El vinilo nunca muere Client: Fnac

"The old rockers never die", is what the old school romantics usually say. "Vinyl neither", we said, when it came to putting together the Fnac campaign to launch their new vinyl section. Adopting the same idealistic spirit typical of the golden age of vinyl, we managed to bring back three great rock stars: Jim Morrison, Janis Joplin and Elvis Presley. How?, by using vinyl coverings in which their faces play the leading roles and making them coincide with the bodies of three models. So, with a play on perspectives, it is the singers who appear to be doing the posing. The final conclusion: "Fnac revives a music legend. Vinyl".

"Los viejos rockeros nunca mueren", suelen decir los románticos de la vieja escuela. "Pues, el vinilo tampoco", nos dijimos nosotros, a la hora de crear la campaña de la Fnac para anunciar su nueva sección de vinilos. Adoptando el espíritu idealista tan propio de la época dorada del vinilo, conseguimos resucitar a tres grandes del rock: Jim Morrison, Janis Joplin y Elvis Presley. ¿Cómo?, usando portadas de vinilos donde sus caras son las protagonistas y haciéndolas coincidir con los cuerpos de tres modelos. Así, con el juego de perspectivas, los que parecen posar son los cantantes. El cierre, clarificador, concluye: "La Fnac resucita a una leyenda de la música. El vinilo".

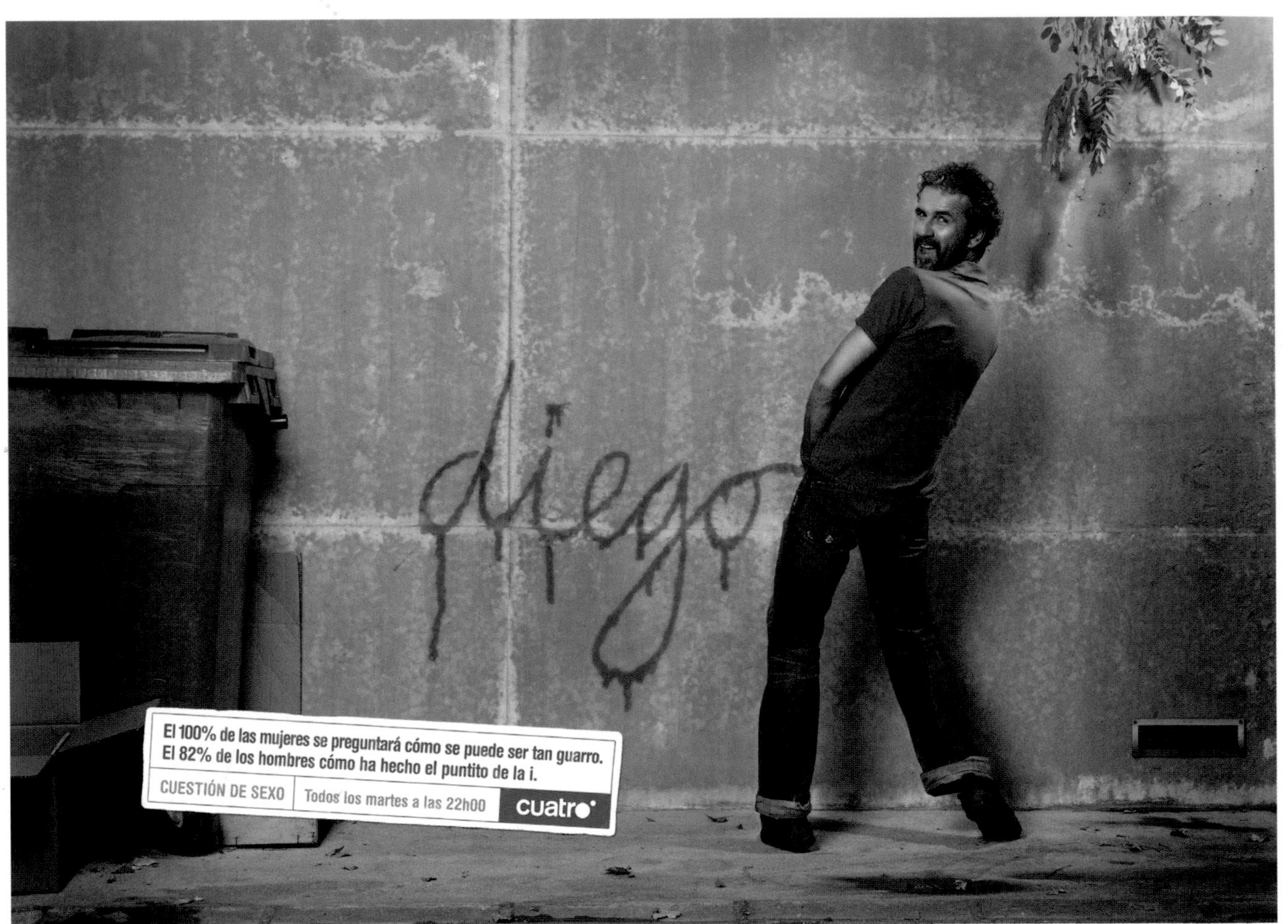

Campaing: Cuestión de sexo Client: Cadena CUATRO

El 80% de las mujeres verá a una madre con un niño.
El 100% de los hombres no sabrá de qué niño hablamos.
CUESTIÓN DE SEXO
Todos los martes a las 22h00
cuatro

Reg. Charity No. 216250 and SC037605.You must be over 18. Standard text message costs apply. Because of the sensitive subject matter we have used an actor.

He went to school.
He got expelled.
He went to school.
He got expelled.
He went to school.
He got expelled.
He came to us.
He didn't.

Sometimes the buck passing has to stop. The troubled teenager will never get his life back on track if he keeps getting kicked out of school. What he needs is stability, and that's where we come in. If children with educational difficulties are referred to Barnardo's we stick by them. We work closely with their teachers and families. We help them fulfil their potential through a wide range of projects. And when we do part company with them, hopefully it's only to get them back into school.

Believe in children
Barnardo's

BBH is a full-service agency with an exceptional record of producing creatively-driven communications that build brands. We develop long, mutually-rewarding relationships with our clients and are proud to be working with two of our founding clients –Audi and Levi's –26 years on. The Agency specialises in brand strategy and creativity that can exist across all media platforms through the primacy of the idea. Majority privately-owned, BBH is admired and respected by its peers, the industry and clients alike for its integrity and relentless pursuit of creative excellence.

BBH es una agencia de servicio integral con una trayectoria excepcional en la producción de comunicaciones creativas para la consolidación de marcas. Desarrollamos relaciones largas y mutuamente provechosas con nuestros clientes y estamos orgullosos de estar trabajando con dos de nuestros clientes fundadores, Audi y Levi's, 26 años más tarde. La Agencia se especializa en el desarrollo de estrategias de marca y creatividad que pueden existir en todas las plataformas de medios. BBH es principalmente de propiedad privada, y es admirada y respetada por sus pares, por la industria y por los clientes por su integridad y su búsqueda implacable de la excelencia creativa.

Reg. Charity No. 216250 and SC037605. You must be over 18. Standard text message costs apply. Because of the sensitive subject matter we have used an actor.
He told his parents to f**k off. He told his foster parents to f**k off. He told fourteen social workers to f**k off. He told us to f**k off. But we didn't. And we still haven't.
There are thousands of disadvantaged children in the UK. Many of them have stories that would break your heart. Some of them are capable of terrible things. But if, like us, you believe that no child is born bad, then you can't watch someone get dumped into the file marked 'problem'. You can't let society play pass the parcel with a young person's life. If a child is referred to Barnardo's we stick by that child. We listen. We look for potential. We give practical support. And if we don't give up on the troubled, young boy, it's not because we enjoy being sworn at, it's because we believe in him.
Believe in children
Barnardo's

Campaing: Never Give Up Client: Barnardo's

This Barnardo's campaign launched the new line, "Believe in Children", which is the Client's new long-term strategic brand positioning, aiming to re-enforce Barnardo's underlying philosophy: that it tirelessly supports the UK's most vulnerable children. The campaign aims to challenge the public's current somewhat negative perception of childhood in the UK today whilst inspiring them to support the charity's work. This campaign existed in cinema, online viral, online interactive, outdoor and poster formats.

Esta campaña de Barnardo, lanzó el nuevo mensaje "Believe in Children" ("Cree en los niños"), que es la nueva estrategia a largo plazo de posicionamiento de la marca del cliente, cuyo objetivo es reforzar la filosofía subyacente de Barnardo: que apoya incansablemente a los niños más vulnerables del Reino Unido. La campaña quiere cambiar la percepción negativa de la infancia que se tiene actualmente en el Reino Unido al mismo tiempo que anima a colaborar con su trabajo de caridad. Esta campaña está presente en el cine, periódicos, en la calle, marketing viral, online.

To show you
believe in children,
text 'Believe'
to 84862 or visit
barnardos.org.uk

Would you desert the drowning child or the infant trapped in a fire? How about the angry, inarticulate thief?

Time is running out for thousands of vulnerable children. Society wants to punish them for their crimes, label them 'problems', without any understanding of their circumstances. We, at Barnardos, want to help them. By listening. By offering advice and practical support. And by sticking by them, until they get their troubled, young lives back on the rails.

Believe in children

Barnardo's

To show you
believe in children,
text 'Believe'
to 84862 or visit
barnardos.org.uk

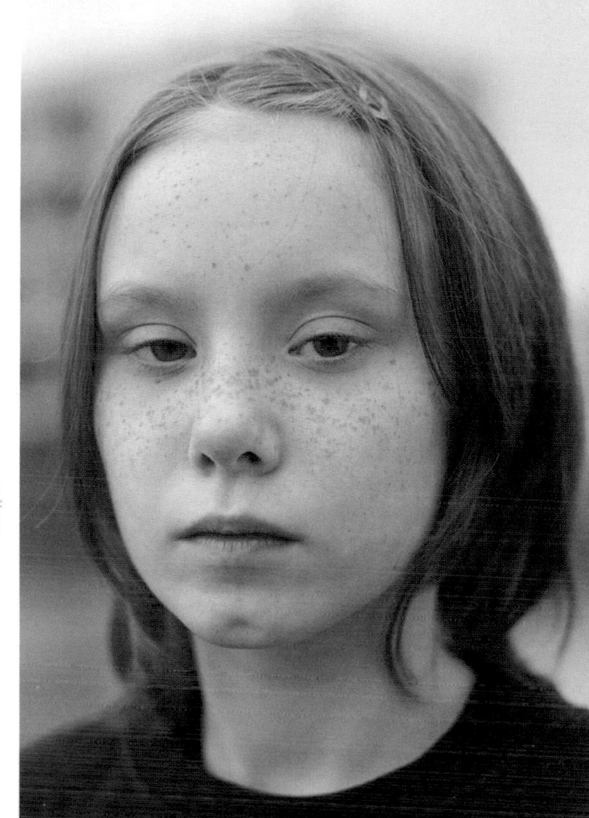

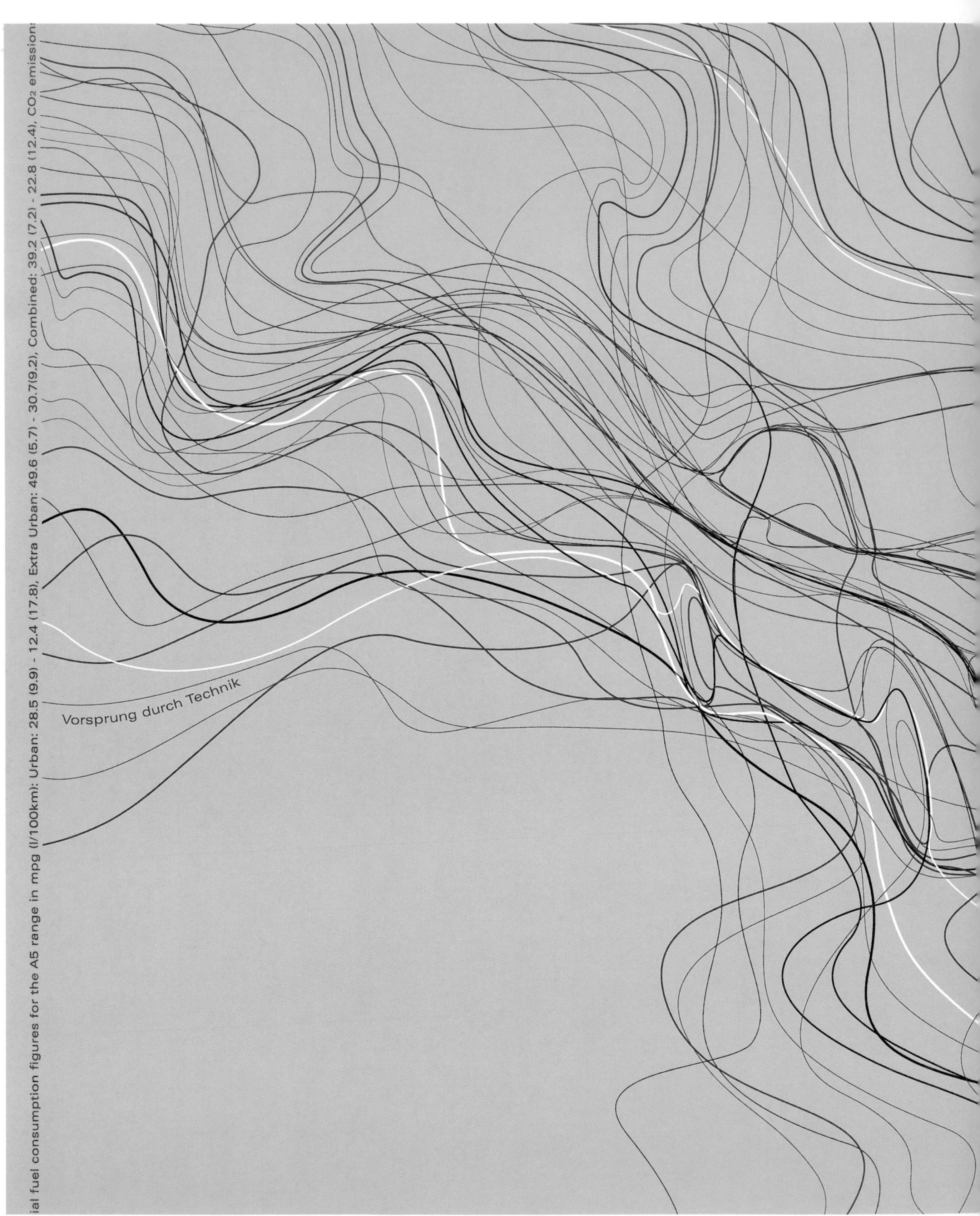
ial fuel consumption figures for the A5 range in mpg (l/100km): Urban: 28.5 (9.9) - 12.4 (17.8), Extra Urban: 49.6 (5.7) - 30.7(9.2), Combined: 39.2 (7.2) - 22.8 (12.4), CO2 emission
Vorsprung durch Technik

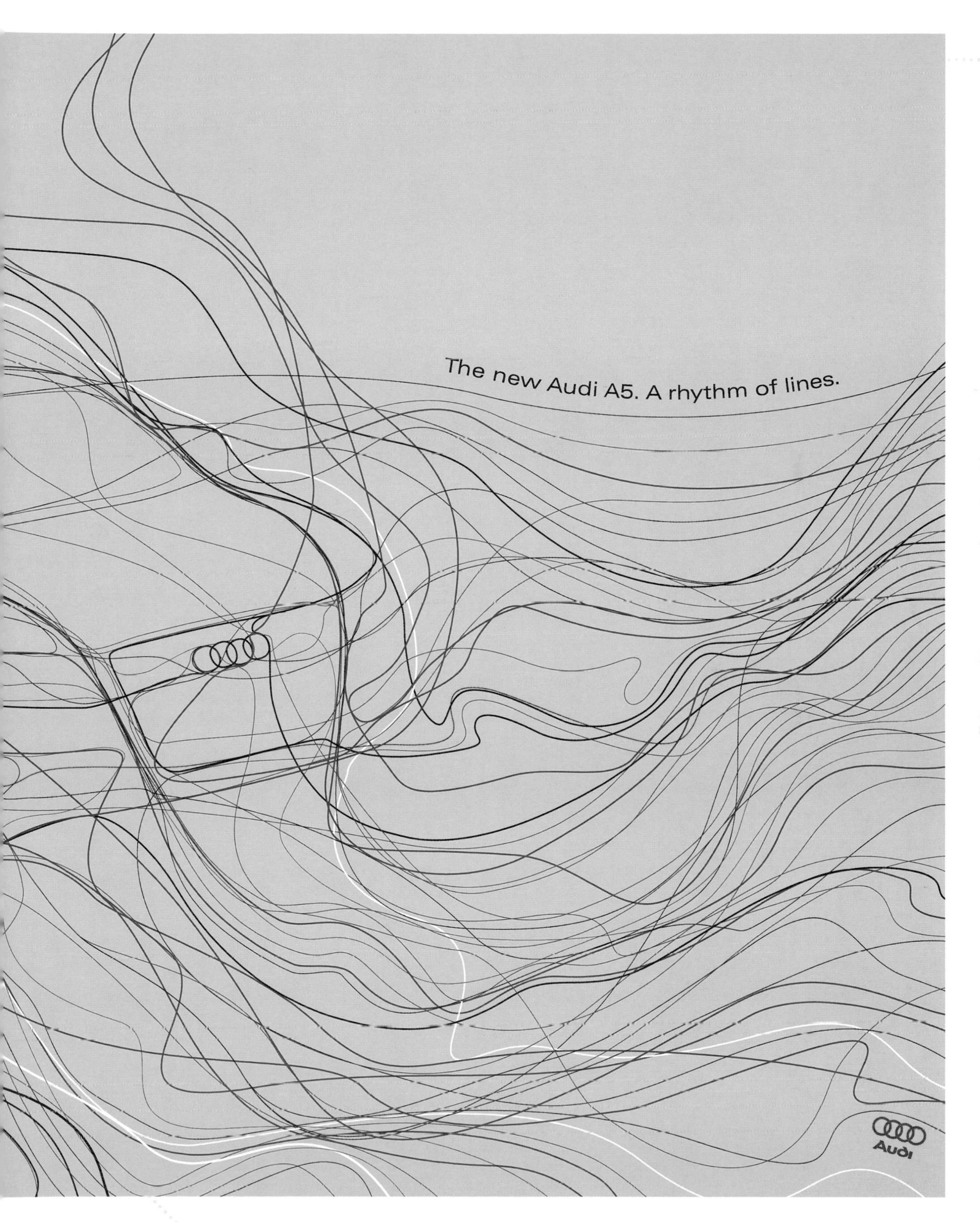
The new Audi A5. A rhythm of lines.
Audi

Campaing: Make the Most of Now Client: Vodafone UK

vodafone

Show work who's the daddy

Mobile Broadband and email

Make the most of now

The new Audi A5. A rhythm of lines.

Audi

Vorsprung durch Technik

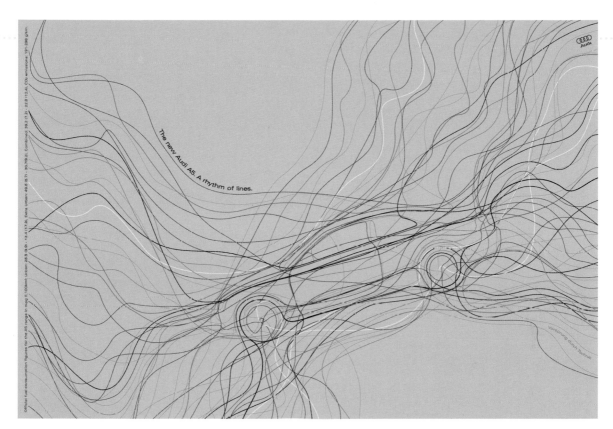

Campaing: A5 Rhythm of Lines Client. Audi

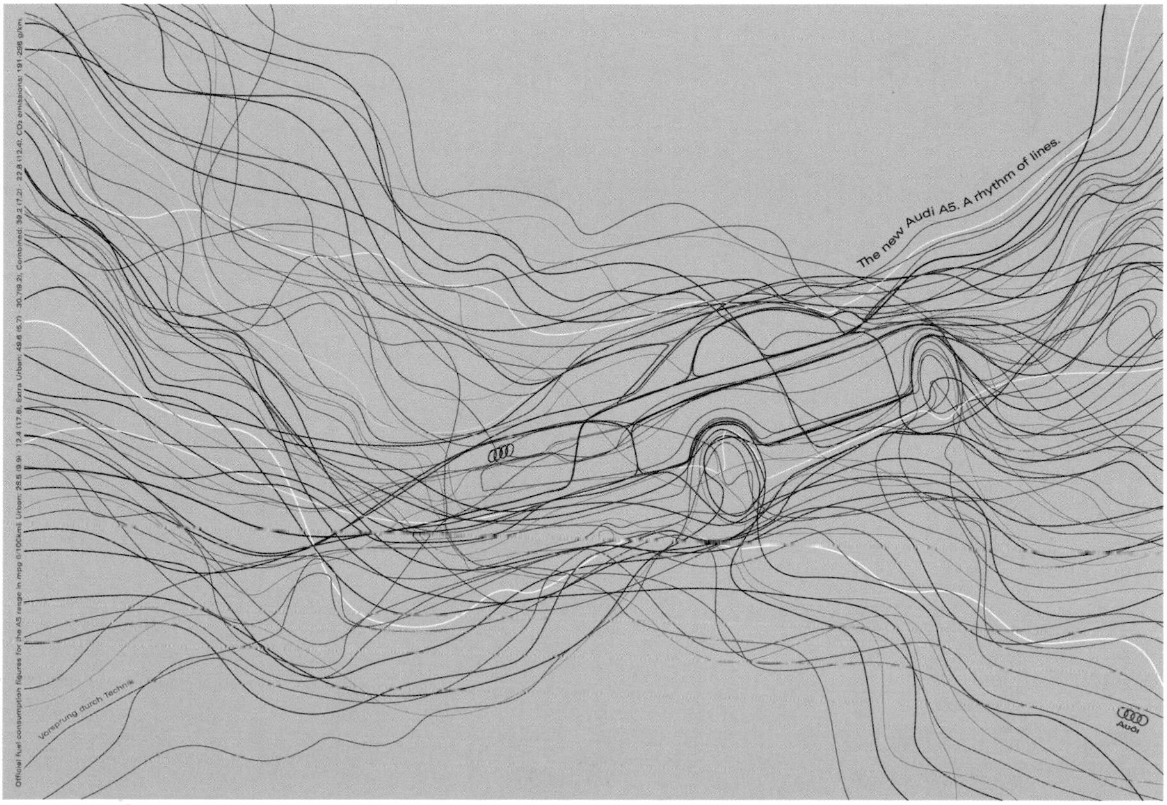

The new Audi A5. A rhythm of lines.

Vorsprung durch Technik

Audi

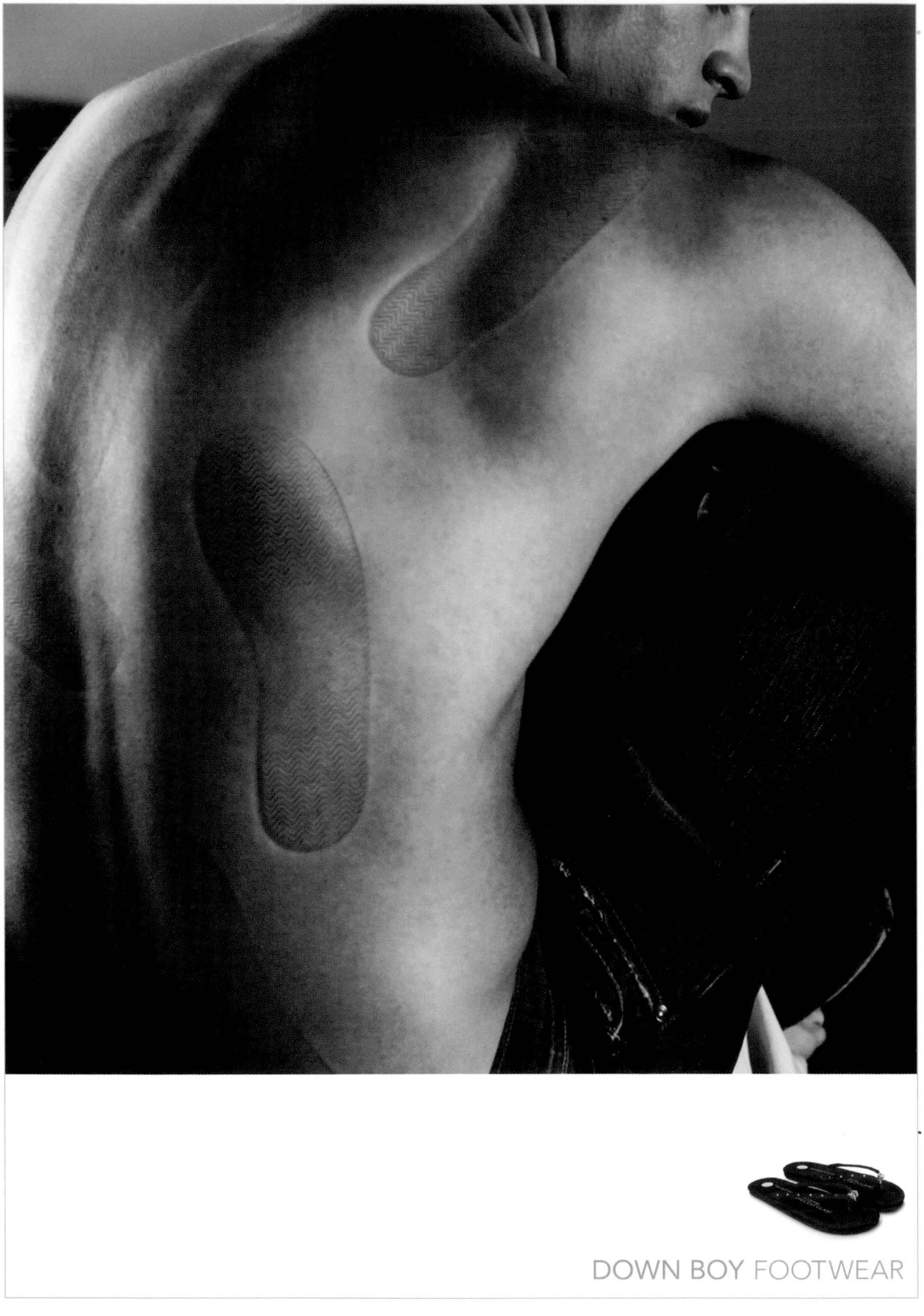

DOWN BOY FOOTWEAR

rethink advertising

Campaing: Down boy Client: Footwear

Rethink was founded in November, 1999 by Chris Staples, Tom Shepansky, and Ian Grais.
Now there are more than 60 Rethinkers, not counting our office dog Bruce. There are also more Rethink partners-five to be exact, including a writer, an art director, an account director, our production manager and our office manager. We are 100-percent owned by our partners. Our core belief is that a great idea can change everything. It can get people talking. It can break through the clutter. It can get results for our clients. We've created campaigns for clients large and small, locally and nationally. For some, we handle all of their advertising and design needs. Others hire us on a project basis.

Rethink fue fundada en noviembre de 1999 por Chris Staples, Tom Shepansky e Ian Grais.
Actualmente hay más de 60 Rethinkers, sin contar el perro de la oficina, Bruce. También hay más socios de Rethink, cinco para ser exactos: un escritor, un director artístico, un director de cuentas, nuestro gerente de producción y nuestro gerente de oficina. Somos propiedad al 100% de nuestros socios.
Nuestra creencia principal es que una gran idea puede cambiarlo todo. Puede hacer que la gente hable. Puede abrirse camino entre el desorden. Puede conseguir resultados para nuestros clientes. Hemos creado campañas para clientes grandes y pequeños, local e internacionalmente. Algunos clientes nos encargan todas sus necesidades de publicidad y de diseño. Otros clientes nos encargan proyectos concretos.

Campaing: BARE Client: BARE

WITH THE WIDEST RANGE OF SIZES ANYWHERE, YOU'LL FIND THE PERFECT FIT RIGHT
OFF THE RACK. BECAUSE WHEN YOU'RE COMFORTABLE, YOU CAN STAY DOWN
BARE
FIT IS EVERYTHING

BARE
WHEN YOU'RE COMFORTABLE, YOU CAN STAY DOWN LONGER. THAT'S WHY OUR SUITS ARE MADE WITH THE
MOST ADVANCED MATERIALS AND TECHNOLOGY, SO YOU'LL FIND THE PERFECT FIT RIGHT OFF THE RACK.

Campaing: Sirius Client: Sirius

102
HAMILTON
TIGER CATS
SEASON TICKETS
604
589-ROAR
bclions.com

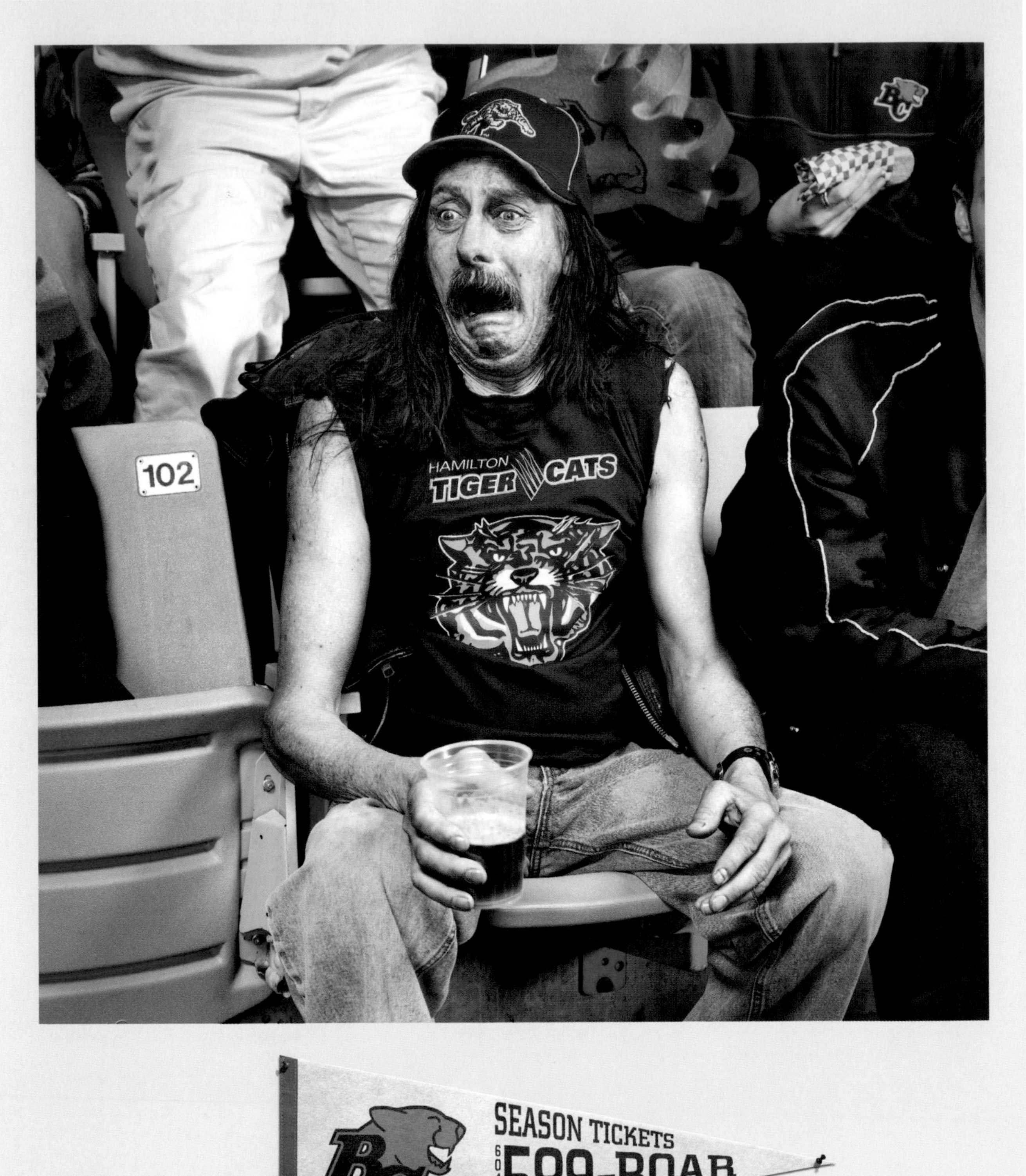

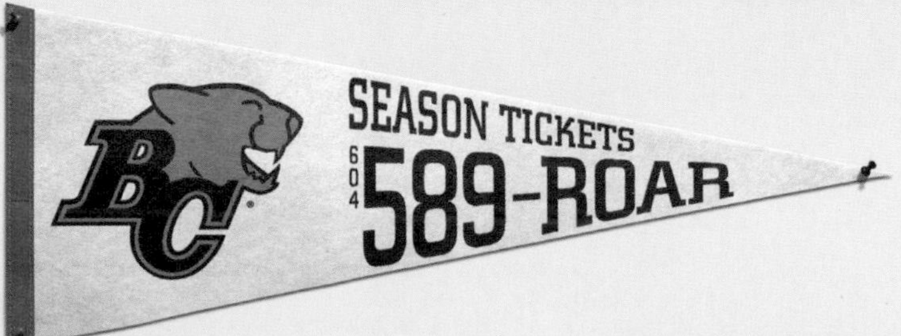

Campaing: BC Lions Client: BC Lions

Established in 1953, the "BC Lions Football Club" began playing in the Canadian Football League (CFL), in the summer of 1954. The CFL consists of eight teams all vying for the Grey Cup title each November.

The BC Lions have experienced a strong resurgence over past several years culminating with winning the Grey Cup in 2006. Average home game attendance had increased from 18,500 in 2002 to over 32,000 in 2005.

Research showed that football fans love the hard-hitting action combined with rivalries between other cities. Many of these rivalries are long-held and passed down through generations. Our print strategy focused on those inter-league rivalries with seven different ads, each showing a dejected rival fan of another CFL team.

The print campaign ran in newspapers, transit stations and at BC Place Stadium.

Fundado en 1953, el "BC Lions Football Club" empezó a jugar en la Liga de Fútbol Canadiense (CFL), en el verano de 1954. En la CFL, ocho equipos compiten por conseguir el título de la Grey Cup cada noviembre.

Los BC Lions han experimentado un fuerte resurgimiento en los últimos años que culminó con la obtención de la Grey Cup en 2006. La asistencia media al campo aumentó de 18.500 en 2002 a más de 32.000 en 2005.

Un estudió mostró que a los aficionados al fútbol les encanta la acción contundente combinada con la rivalidad entre otras ciudades. Muchas de estas rivalidades son muy antiguas y pasan de generación en generación. Nuestra estrategia de publicidad impresa se centró en estas rivalidades con siete anuncios distintos, y en cada uno de ellos aparece un aficionado abatido de otro equipo rival de la CFL.

La campaña impresa apareció en periódicos, estaciones de autobus y en el BC Place Stadium.

Campaing: BC Lions Client: BC Lions

Campaing: BC Lions Client: BC Lions

Clockwise from above: The Monkees; Pat Boone; Ethel Merman; Petula Clark; John Denver; The Everly Brothers. If this sounds right, you need to see Linda McCartney's Sixties: Portrait of an Era. December 1 through January 31, 2006.

1. Jerry Garcia
2. Some Guy
3. Bob Something
4. Keyboard Player
5. Some Other Guy
6. No Idea

REFRESH YOUR MEMORY. **LINDA McCARTNEY'S SIXTIES: PORTRAIT OF AN ERA.** DECEMBER 1 THROUGH JANUARY 31. ROYAL BC MUSEUM

Pictured L to R: If you're reading this, you really need to see Linda McCartney's Sixties: Portrait of an Era. December 1 through January 31.

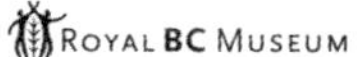

Campaing: Royal BC Museum Client: Royal BC Museum

Campaing: Play Land Client: Play and Land

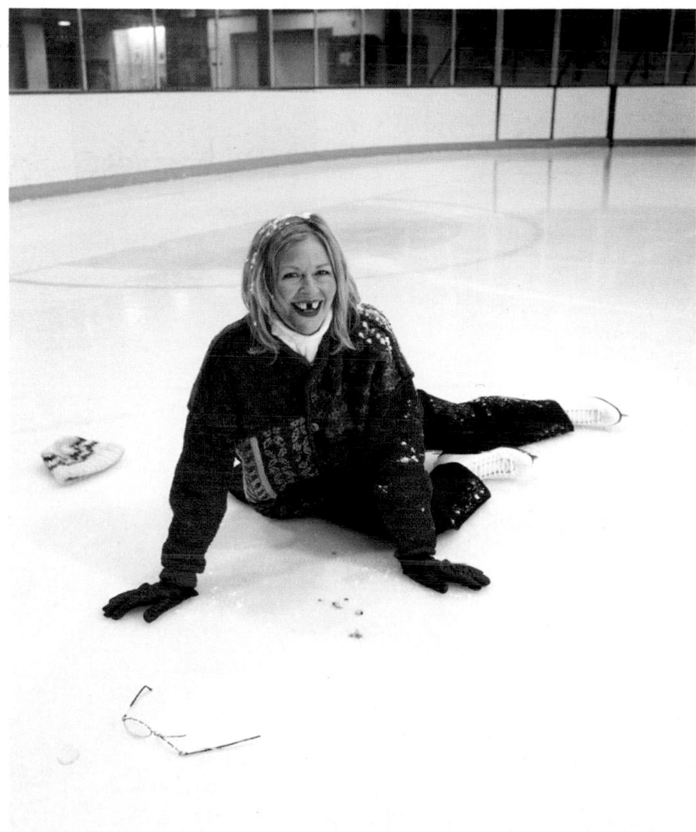

LIFE'S GREAT WHEN YOU HAVE THE RIGHT COVERAGE.
For health and dental insurance, come to us for expert advice. Visit bcaa.com.

Campaing: BCAA Client: BCAA

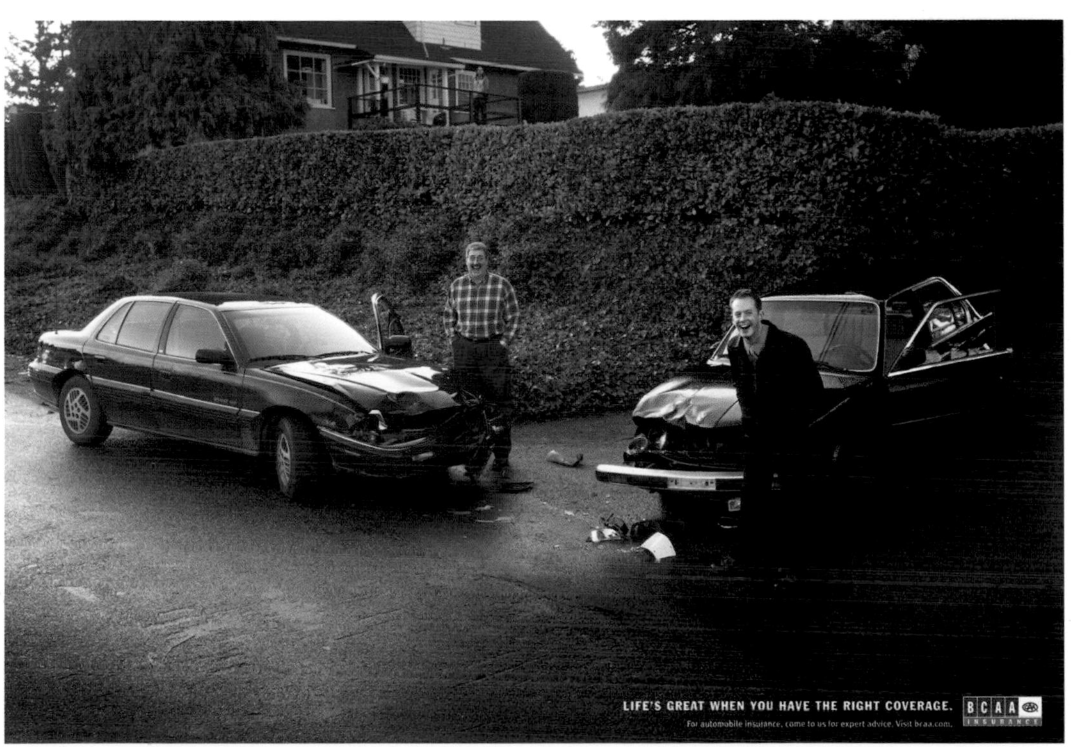

LIFE'S GREAT WHEN YOU HAVE THE RIGHT COVERAGE.
For automobile insurance, come to us for expert advice. Visit bcaa.com.
BCAA
INSURANCE

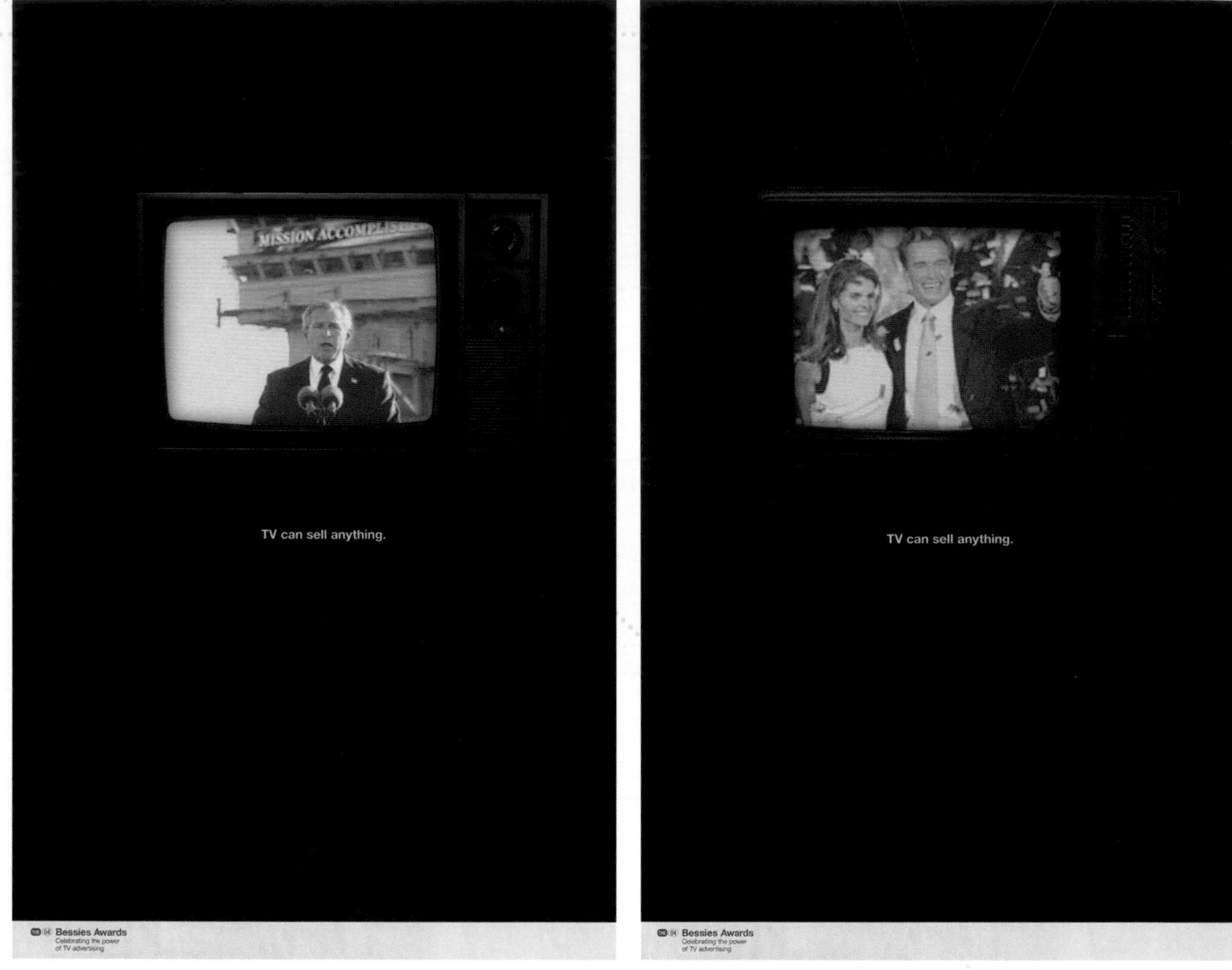
MISSION ACCOMPLISHED
TV can sell anything.
Bessies Awards
Celebrating the power
of TV advertising
TV can sell anything.
Bessies Awards
Celebrating the power
of TV advertising

Campaing: TV can sell anything Client: Bessies Awards

TV can sell anything.

FOX
HOUSE
ESTREIA 4ª TEMPORADA
SEGUNDA DIA 7 DE JAN ÀS
FOX

Campaing: Fox - House Client: FOX Channels

TORKE

Torke is a special agency:
- We have people working in the agency.
- Torke's accounts go to meetings with clients.
- The clients send creative briefings.
- We have computers.
- The creatives think.
- The planners plan.
- Sometimes the coffee gets cold.
- The client receives an e-mail with creative proposals.
- The production department makes the budget.
- The supplyer suplies.
- The creatives talk with their friends.
- Computer mouse makes: Click.
- The accounts go to parties with clients.
- The financial department sends the invoice.
- Sometimes the clients pay on time.

Besides everything else, Torke is quite normal.

P.S. Torke is the first guerrilla marketing agency in Lisbon, Portugal. Our work consists of creating a new approach in terms of brand communications and therefore a different relationship between brands and consumers.

Torke es una agencia especial:
- Tenemos gente trabajando en la agencia.
- Los ejecutivos de cuentas de Torke van a las reuniones con los clientes.
- Los clientes envían briefings creativos.
- Tenemos ordenadores.
- Los creativos piensan.
- Los planificadores planifican.
- El café a veces se enfría.
- El cliente recibe un email con propuestas creativas.
- El departamento de producción hace el presupuesto.
- El proveedor suministra.
- Los creativos hablan con sus amigos.
- El ratón del ordenador hace: Clic.
- Los ejecutivos de cuentas van a fiestas con los clientes.
- El departamento de contabilidad envía la factura.
- A veces los clientes pagan a tiempo.

Por lo demás, Torke es bastante normal.

P.D. Torke es la primera agencia de marketing de guerrilla de Lisboa, Portugal. Nuestro trabajo consiste en crear un nuevo enfoque en términos comunicaciones de marca y por lo tanto, una relación distinta entre marcas y consumidores.

Campaing: NGC - Martial Arts Client: NGC Channels

In order to promote the Martial Arts Week by the National Geographic Channel (NGC) –a series of documentaries about the surprising Martial Arts –a press kit constituted by a brick, a black belt and a leaflet was sent to the press and media buyers with information about the series and the programme schedule. The press kit defies whoever opens it to try and break the brick, making that person feel like a true Martial Art Master.

For the final consumer about 150 black belts and flyers were placed in different supports throughout the city of Lisbon.

Con la intención de promocionar la Semana de las Artes Marciales emitida por el National Geographic Channel (NGC), una serie de documentales sobre el sorprendente mundo de las Artes Marciales, se envió un kit de prensa formado por un ladrillo, un cinturón negro y un folleto con información sobre la serie y el calendario del programa. El kit de prensa reta a quien lo abra, a intentar romper el ladrillo, haciendo que esa persona se sienta como un verdadero Maestro de las Artes Marciales.

Para el consumidor final, se colocaron 150 cinturones negros y flyers en distintos puntos de la ciudad de Lisboa.

Campaing: Desperated Housewives Client: FOX Channels

In order to communicate the premiere on FOX of the 2nd season of Desperated Housewives, in Lisbon 14 people walked around the city in the day-by-day routes with a cartoon like thought baloon with the copy: "Can't forget: Premiere of Desperated Housewives", with the day and time of the premiere.
This campaign was covered by the major national newspapers.

Para comunicar el estreno en la FOX de la 2ª temporada de Mujeres Desesperadas, 14 personas se pasearon por la ciudad de Lisboa día tras día con un globo en forma de viñeta que decía: "No te olvides: Estreno de Mujeres Desesperadas", con el día y la hora del estreno.
Esta campaña fue cubierta por los principales periódicos nacionales.

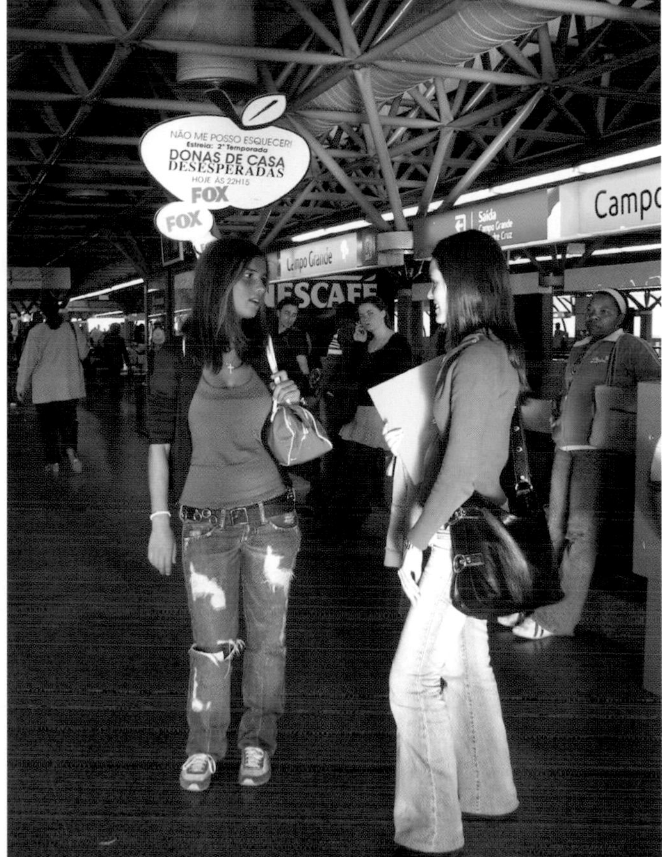

Campaing: Prision Break Client: FOX Channels

In order to launch the TV series Prison Break on the Portuguese FOX Channel, a multi-phased advertising campaign was performed in Lisbon:

1- Press/Kit

A book containing a hidden spoon and a prison blueprint was sent to the press relating to a prison escape, the TV Show main theme. Inside the book was a CD containing info abou the TV show.

2- Street Campaign: Prisoners

A team of 7 people (5 prisoners and 2 policemen) walked throughout the city of Lisbon distributing flyers containing info about the TV Show.

3- Street Campaign: Posters

Several posters behind bars, illustrating the prison were strategically placed in various city areas.

Para lanzar la serie de TV Prison Break en el canal FOX portugués, se realizó una campaña publicitaria de varias fases en Lisboa:

1- Kit de prensa

Se envió a la prensa un libro que contenía una cuchara oculta y un plano de la prisión en referencia a la fuga, el tema principal de la serie. Dentro del libro había un CD con información sobre el programa.

2- Campaña en la calle: Prisioneros

Un equipo de 7 personas (5 prisioneros y 2 policías) se paseó por la ciudad de Lisboa distribuyendo pósteres con información sobre el programa.

3- Campaña de en la calle: Póster

Se colocaron varios pósteres detrás de rejas, representando la prisión, en varias zonas de la ciudad.

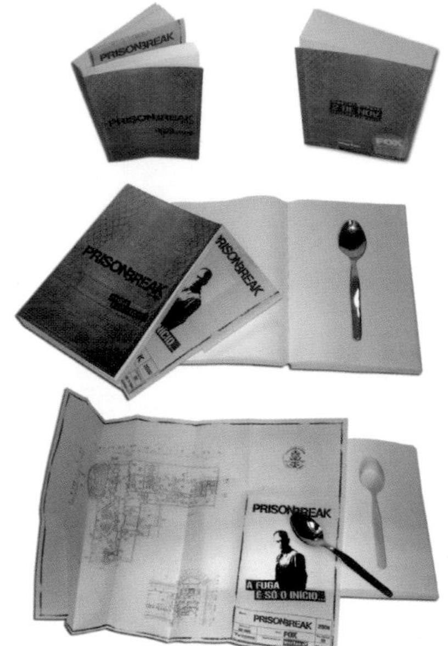

Campaing: Peugeot 308 Client: Peugeot

In order to prommote the launch of a new model: 308. This campaign was divided in two different actions:

1- Truck

As a Teaser to promote the launching of the new Peugeot 308, two vehicle-transport trucks circulated trhoughout the country, carrying three giant "308" logotypes, matching the size of the car; and the text "It's arriving!". The trucks stopped by the Peugeot dealers, enticing the curiosity of those passing by, and creating a rush of "word-of-mouth" about Peugeot's new car.

2- Boxes

58 wooden boxes were "parked" in the main Portuguese cities –including the Azores and Madeira Islands. Built to match the 308 size, these boxes were made to entice the curiosity of the people passing by. A hole teased people to peep through it. Inside, a message invited everyone to go to nearest Peugeot dealer, after the launching.

Para promocionar el lanzamiento del nuevo modelo 308 se realizó una campaña dividida en dos acciones distintas:

1- Camión

Como avance para promocionar el lanzamiento del nuevo Peugeot 308, dos camiones de transporte de vehículos circularon por todo el país, con tres logotipos "308" gigantes, del tamaño del coche, y el mensaje: "¡Ya llega!". Los camiones se detuvieron en los concesionarios Peugeot, atrayendo la curiosidad de los pasantes, y generando un torrente de comentarios "boca a boca" sobre el nuevo coche de Peugeot.

2- Cajas

Se "aparcaron" 58 cajas de madera en las principales ciudades portuguesas, incluidas las islas Azores y Madeira. Estas cajas, que tenían el mismo tamaño que el 308, se construyeron con el objetivo de atraer la curiosidad de la gente que pasa por ahí. Dentro de ellas, un mensaje invitaba a todo el mundo a acercarse al concesionario Peugeot más cercano después del lanzamiento.

Campaing: Fox - House Client: FOX Channels

In order to communicate FOX's 4th Season of House in Portugal, several statues were covered with medical masks containing the info about the premiere.

Para anunciar la 4ª temporada de House en la FOX en Portugal, se cubrieron varias estatuas con máscaras médicas que contenían información sobre el estreno.

00'00"

00'01"

00'09"

BIG STORIES
DON'T NEED A LONG
TIME TO HAPPEN.

SATURDAYS AT 7 PM DURING OCTOBER.

publicis

We believe in stimulating and leading conversations for brands through creating contagious ideas that "echo in the schoolyard".

Founded by Marcel Bleustein-Blanchet in 1926, Publicis Worldwide is built from a strong French heritage and all its best characteristics of style, innovation and passion. Publicis Worldwide is made up of three core brands, Publicis for advertising, Publicis Dialog for marketing services and Publicis Modem for digital giving us the expert capabilities to service a client's communications needs in one truly holistic company. Our global network is actively helping clients initiate conversations with their customers, in any language, anywhere to grow their brands and increase their market share. And in an increasingly cross-border and cross-cultural world our multi-cultural heritage gives us a unique advantage. With a strong presence in 83 countries, 256 offices and 9,000 employees, we are best in class specialists for an evolving communications landscape.

Creemos en las conversaciones estimulantes y punteras para consolidar marcas por medio de la creación de ideas contagiosas que "resuenan en el patio del colegio".

Publicis Worldwide, fundada por Marcel Bleustein-Blanchet en 1926, presenta una fuerte herencia francesa y sus mejores características de estilo, innovación y pasión. Publicis Worldwide está compuesta por tres marcas básicas: Publicis, dedicada a la publicidad, Publicis Dialog, dedicada a servicios de marketing y Publicis Modem, dedicada al marketing digital; dándonos la capacidad para hacernos cargo de las necesidades de comunicación del cliente en una empresa totalmente integral. Nuestra red global ayuda activamente a nuestros clientes a iniciar conversaciones con sus clientes, en cualquier lengua y en cualquier lugar, para consolidar sus marcas y aumentar su participación en el mercado, y en un mundo cada vez más internacional y transcultural, nuestra herencia multicultural nos da una ventaja única. Con una fuerte presencia en 83 países, 256 oficinas y 9.000 empleados, somos especialistas "best in class" en un entorno de comunicaciones en constante evolución.

00'00"
02'07"
02'56"
BIG STORIES
DON'T NEED A LONG
TIME TO HAPPEN.
AXN
SHORT FILM
FESTIVAL
2006
SATURDAYS AT 7 PM DURING OCTOBER.

Campaing: Short film festival 06 Client: AXN

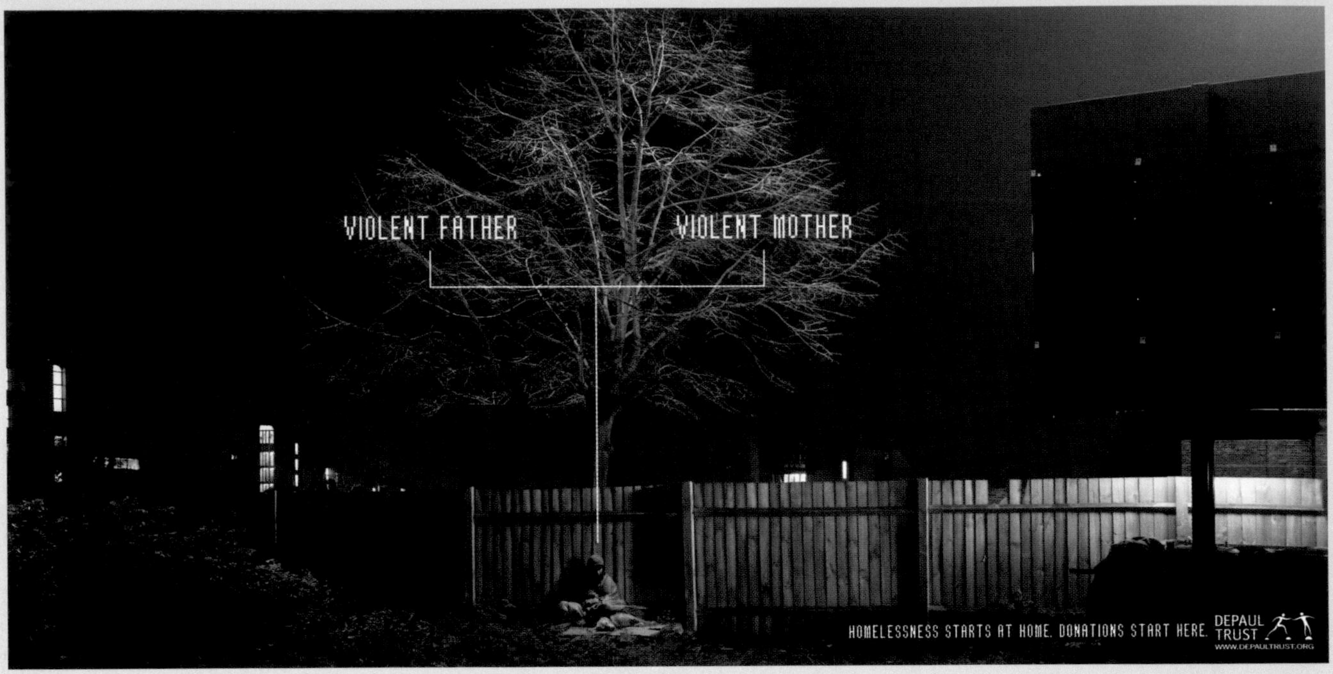

VIOLENT FATHER
VIOLENT MOTHER
HOMELESSNESS STARTS AT HOME. DONATIONS START HERE.
DEPAUL TRUST
WWW.DEPAULTRUST.ORG

Campaing: Depaul Trust Client: Depaul Trust

MOTHER DIED
FATHER DRANK
HOMELESSNESS STARTS AT HOME. DONATIONS S

PROSTITUTE MOTHER

FATHER UNKNOWN

HOMELESSNESS STARTS AT HOME. DONA

Campaing: Wonderbra Client: Wonderbra

Two years ago, Wonderbra picked up where it left off in the world of communications, launching a breakout campaign that made people talking!.

After years of mining the possibilities of the unique advertising concept launched years ago with Eva Herzigova, the famous bra brand was back in the publicity spotlight with a campaign developed by Publicis Conseil that breaked with the clichés of the category. In handing over the development of its new advertising strategy to Publicis Conseil, Wonderbra assigned the Agency three objectives:

- Change the brand's image from "a product that makes breasts bigger" to "the brand that makes me sexier".
- Realign Wonderbra with fashion and everyday wear, based on the new existing range of four bras for four types of necklines.
- And especially, recreate a positive buzz around the product, remaking it as a brand that has people talking because it has something different to say.

The strategy selected by Publicis Conseil was simple: to break with the clichés of the category by altering the message, the woman who wears a Wonderbra was still the centre of attention, but this woman could be anyone.

In effect, instead of imposing a model on the reader, the idea consisted of allowing her to directly experience what she would feel when she wears a Wonderbra: sexy, sure of herself and her powers of seduction, and turning all eyes her way.

Hace dos años Wonderbra reanudó su estrategia de comunicación ahí donde la había dejado, lanzando una campaña rompedora que dio mucho que hablar.

Tras años exprimiendo las posibilidades del original concepto publicitario lanzado años atrás con Eva Herzigova, la famosa marca de sujetadores volvió a situarse en el punto de mira de la publicidad con una campaña creada por Publicis Conseil que rompió todos los clichés de la categoría. Cuando Wonderbra le encargó a Publicis Conseil el desarrollo de su nueva estrategia de publicidad, le marcó tres objetivos:

- Cambiar la imagen de la marca, de "un producto que aumenta el tamaño del pecho" a "la marca que me hace más sexy".
- Realinear Wonderbra con la moda y la ropa informal, aprovechando la nueva gama de cuatro sujetadores para cuatro tipos de escote.
- Y especialmente crear una sensación positiva alrededor del producto, mostrándolo como una marca que da que hablar porque tiene algo distinto que decir.

La estrategia seleccionada por Publicis Conseil era simple: romper los clichés de la categoría alterando el mensaje, la mujer que lleva Wonderbra sigue siendo el centro de atención, pero esta mujer podría ser cualquiera.

De hecho, en vez de imponer un modelo en la lectora, la idea consistía en permitirle experimentar directamente como se sentiría al llevar un Wonderbra: sexy, segura de ella misma, de sus poderes de seducción y centro de todas las miradas.

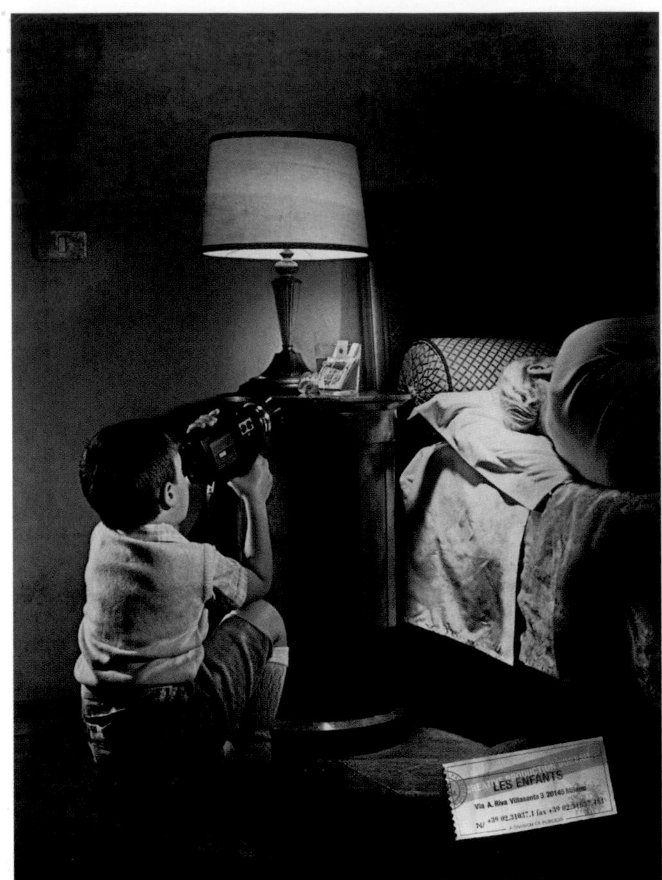

Campaing: Les Enfants Client: Les Enfants

00'00"

00'06"

00'17"

BIG STORIES
DON'T NEED A LONG
TIME TO HAPPEN.

SATURDAYS AT 7 PM DURING OCTOBER.

Campaing: Short film festival 06 Client: AXN

DIESEL
FOR SUCCESSFUL LIVING

Marcel paris

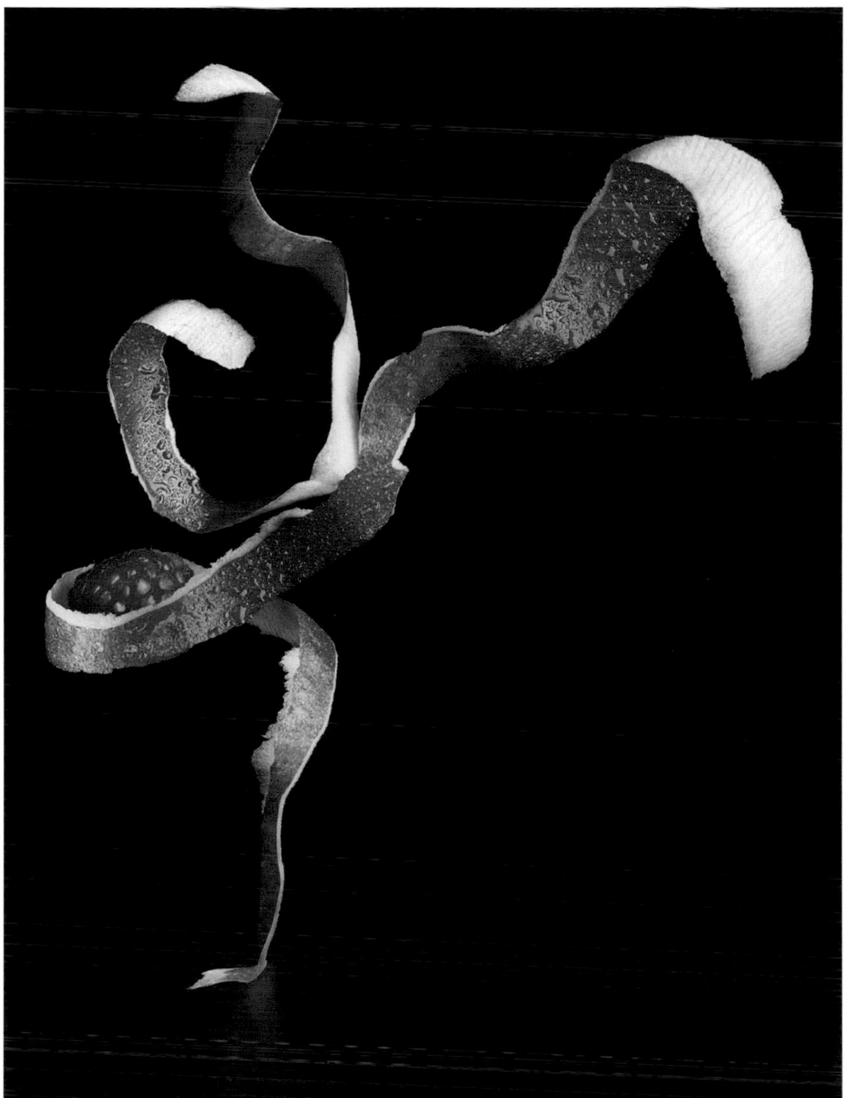

Campaing: Dancer Client: Minute Maid

Campaing: Human after all Client: Diesel

Marcel is an international creative agency belonging to the Publicis Group.
It was first founded in 2005 by Fred & Farid, who left the company in 2006.
The agency is now led by Frederic Temin and Anne de Maupeou, and it's quite an unique example on the French market of an agency led by a team of creatives.
Its clients are, among others, Coca Cola, Diesel, Nestlé Waters, Pernod Ricard, France 24, Canal Jimmy and Comedy.
In 2007 it has been one of the most awarded French agencies, with two Lions in Cannes, three Eurobest, and four Epicas, including the Grand Prix.

Marcel es una agencia creativa internacional que pertenece al Grupo Publicis.
Originalmente fue fundada en 2005 por Fred & Farid, que dejó la empresa en 2006.
Actualmente, la agencia tiene al frente a Frederic Temin y Anne de Maupeou, y es un ejemplo único en el mercado francés de agencia dirigida por un equipo de creativos.
Sus clientes son, entre otros, Coca Cola, Diesel, Nestlé Waters, Pernod Ricard, France 24, Canal Jimmy y Comedy.
En 2007 fue una de las agencias francesas más galardonadas, con dos Leones en Cannes, tres Eurobest, y cuatro Epicas, incluido el Grand Prix.

Campaing: Live fast Client: Diesel

DIESEL
FOR SUCCESSFUL LIVING
live fast

DIESEL
FOR SUCCESSFUL LIVING
live fast

in a series of DIESEL "how to..." guides to successful living. For more information call diesel headquarter +39 0424 477 555 www.diesel.com

DIESEL
FOR SUCCESSFUL LIVING
GLOBAL

Campaing: Global warming ready Client: Diesel

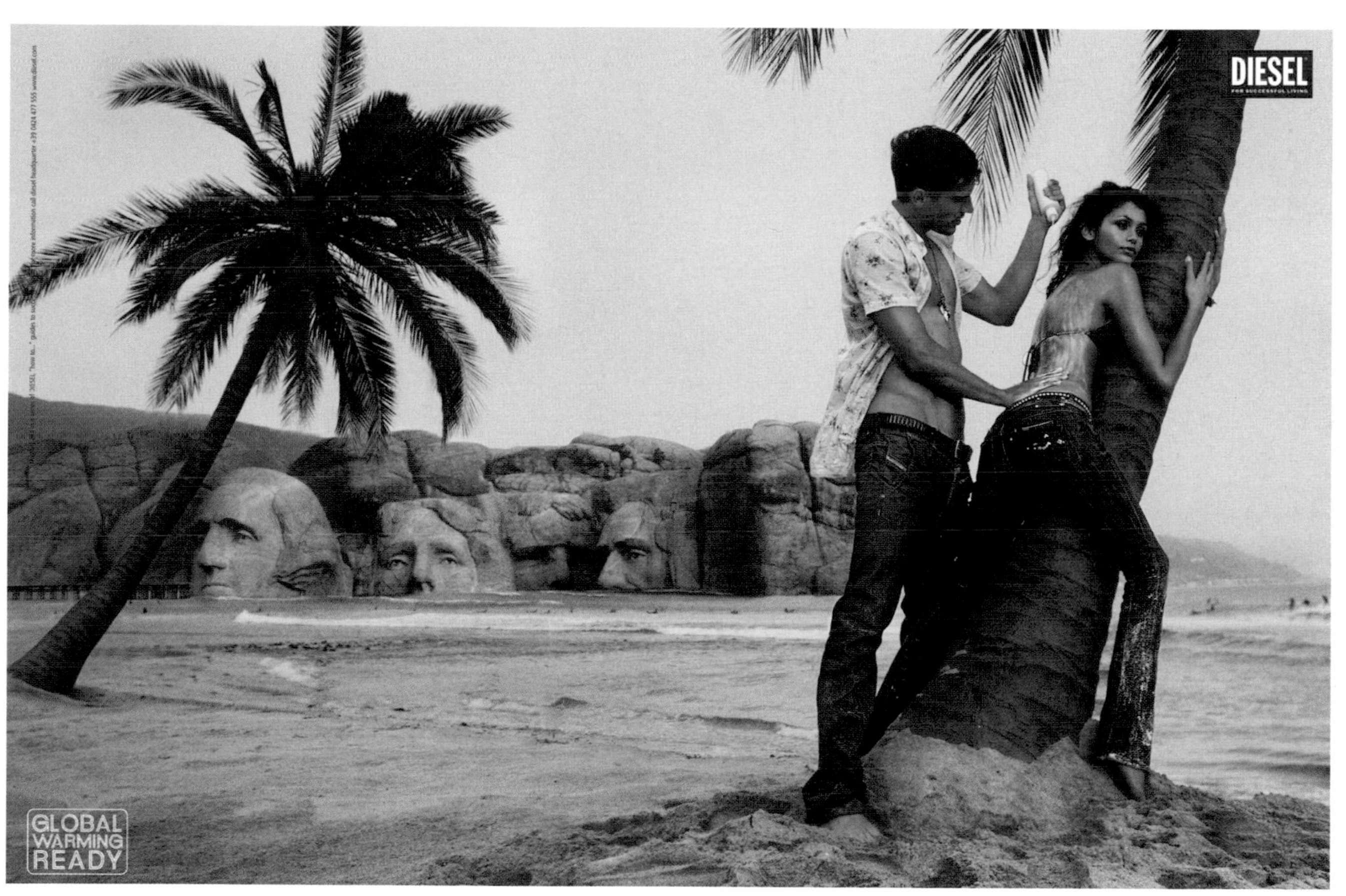

Campaing: Global warming ready Client: Diesel

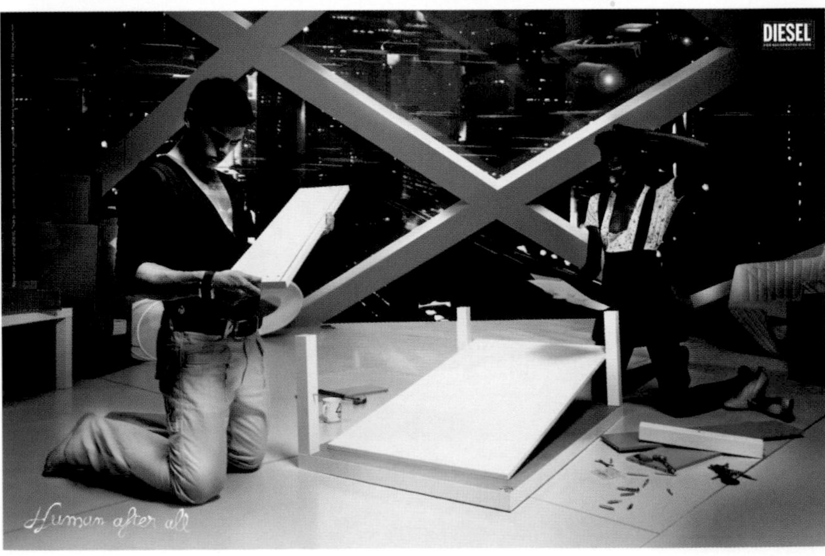

Campaing: Human after all Client: Diesel

Campaing: Human after all Client: Diesel

We don't really know what our future will be made of. Science fiction and dreams fulfill our imagination with intelligent machines, flying cars, time travel, weird genetic engineering, infinite cloning... We expect our lives to change, sometimes for the best, sometimes for the worst. Between hope and fear of the unknown, creatives point out there is one thing left we can count on: us!, all of us fellow human beings!. Good news, whatever our future will be, human beings will be there, and they won't come alone. There's a chance they bring their fascinating human skills with them. After silver lion winning "Global warming ready" campaign, Marcel exposes another social point of view. We are "Human after all", we have these amazing abilities to take a day to assemble a table, to break windows by mistake, to deeply love and hate the same person, and this is not going to change. We are only human beings, right?. Let's keep this way. We are so lovely with all our little human beahviors and miskates.

No sabemos que nos depara el futuro. La ciencia ficción y los sueños alimentan nuestra imaginación con máquinas inteligentes, coches voladores, extraña ingeniería genética, clonación infinita... Esperamos que nuestras vidas cambien, a veces a mejor, a veces a peor. Entre la esperanza y el miedo a lo desconocido, los creativos señalan que hay algo en lo que todavía podemos contar: ¡nosotros mismos!, ¡los seres humanos!. Buenas noticias, sea cual sea nuestro futuro, los seres humanos estaremos ahí, y no estaremos solos.

Hay muchas posibilidades de que traigamos nuestras fascinantes habilidades con nosotros. Después de la campaña "Global warming ready" galardonada con un León de Plata, Marcel expone otro punto de vista social. "Human after all", ("Somos humanos a pesar de todo"), tenemos estas increíbles capacidades para invertir todo un día en montar una mesa, romper ventanas accidentalmente, amar y odiar profundamente a la misma persona y esto no va a cambiar. Solo somos humanos, ¿no?. No dejemos que esto cambie. Somos encantadores con todos nuestros comportamientos y errores humanos.

Minute Maid
1/5
of R.D.I in
vitamin C

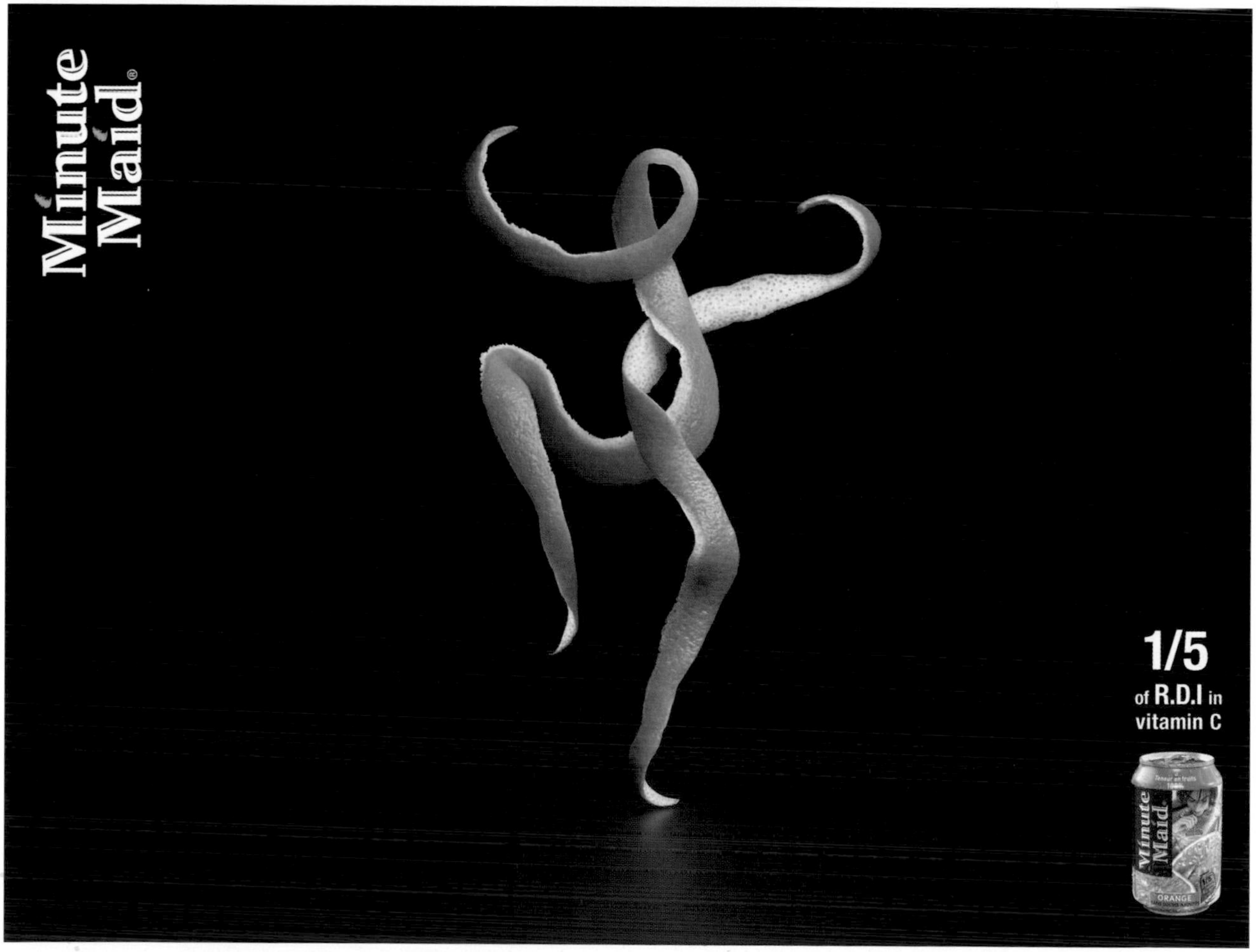

Campaing: Dancer Client: Minute Maid

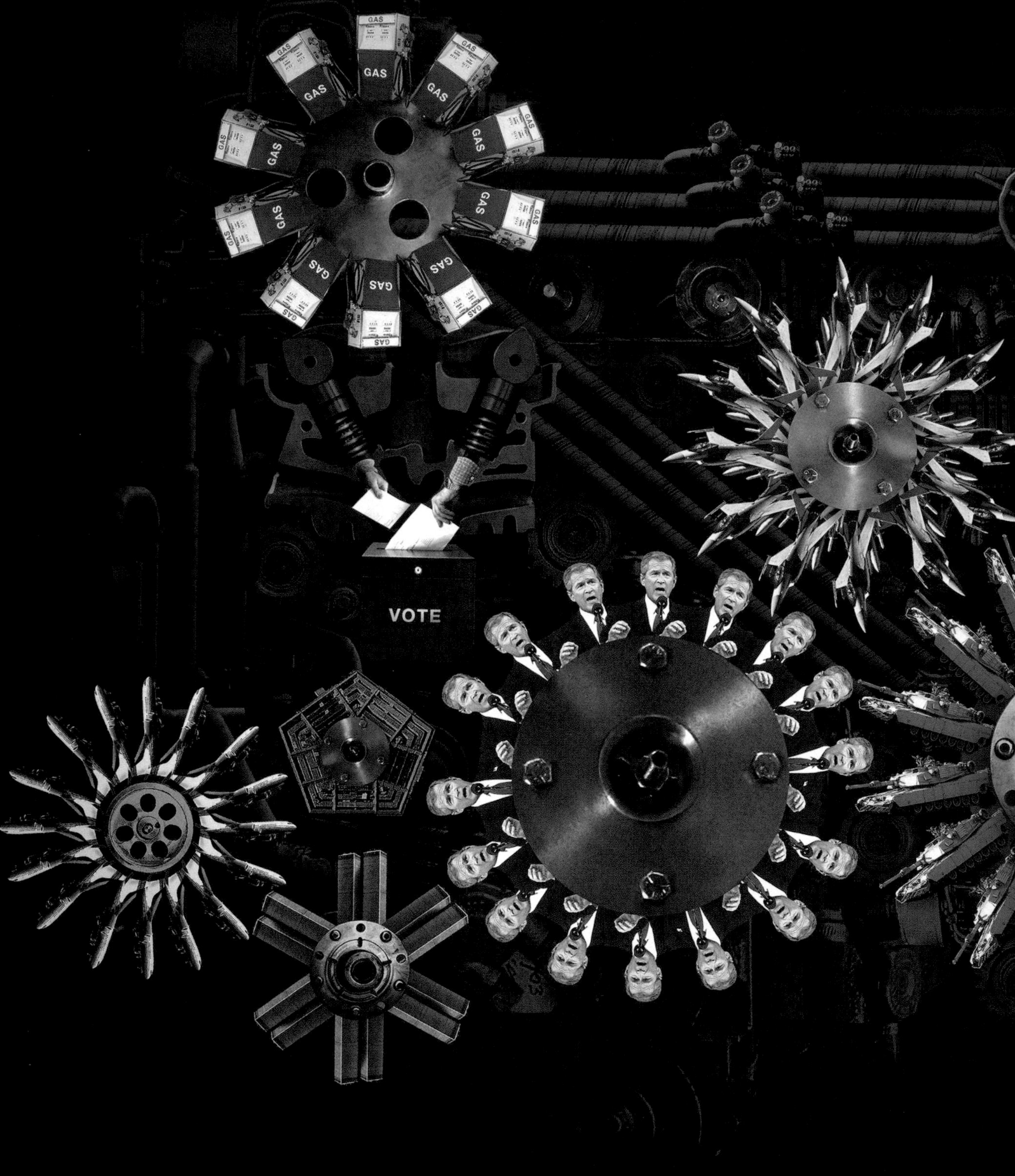
GAS
VOTE

FRANCE
24

Campaing: Beyond the news Client: France 24

Campaing: Beyond the news Client: France 24

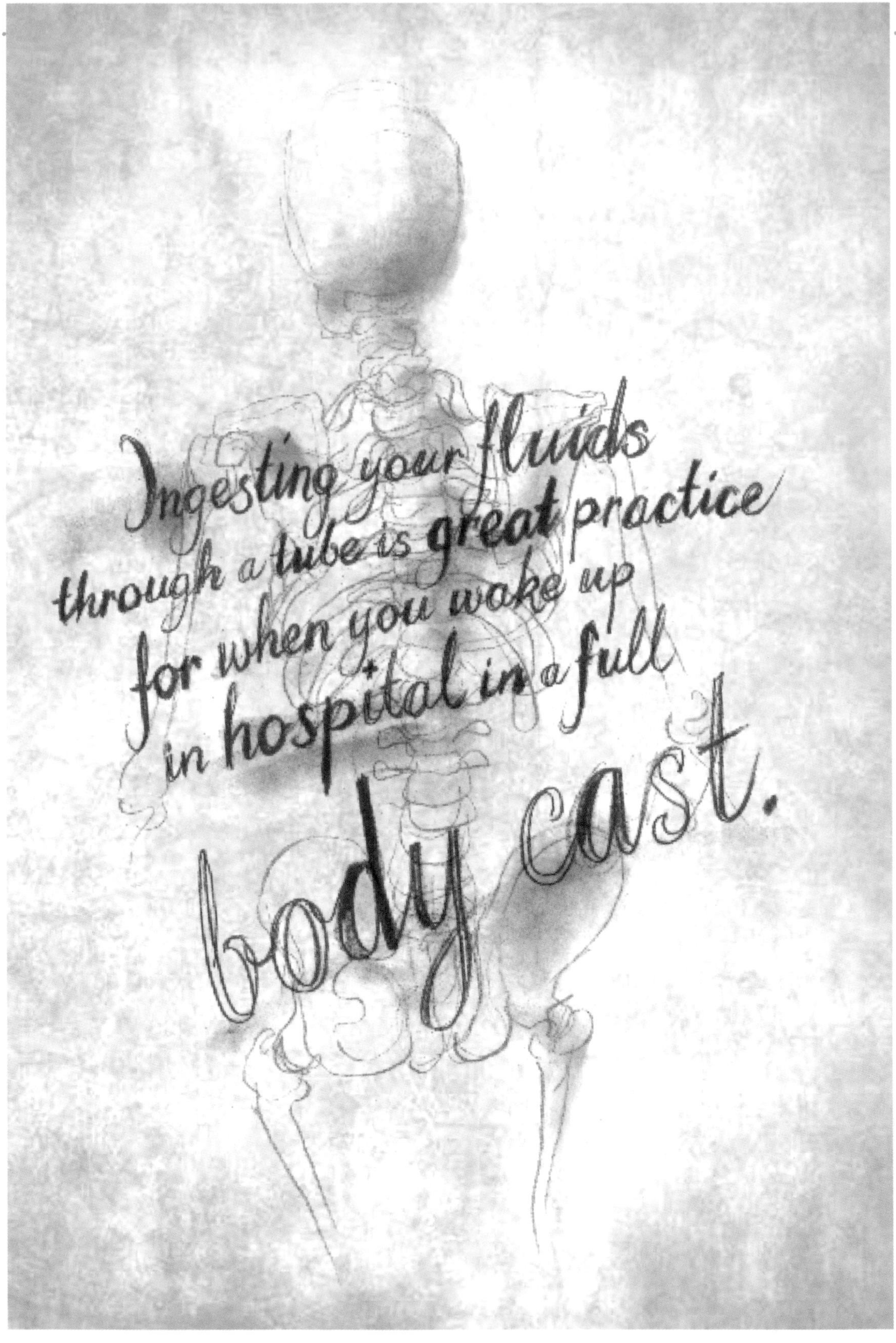

Ingesting your fluids
through a tube is great practice
for when you wake up
in hospital in a full
body cast.

draftfcb

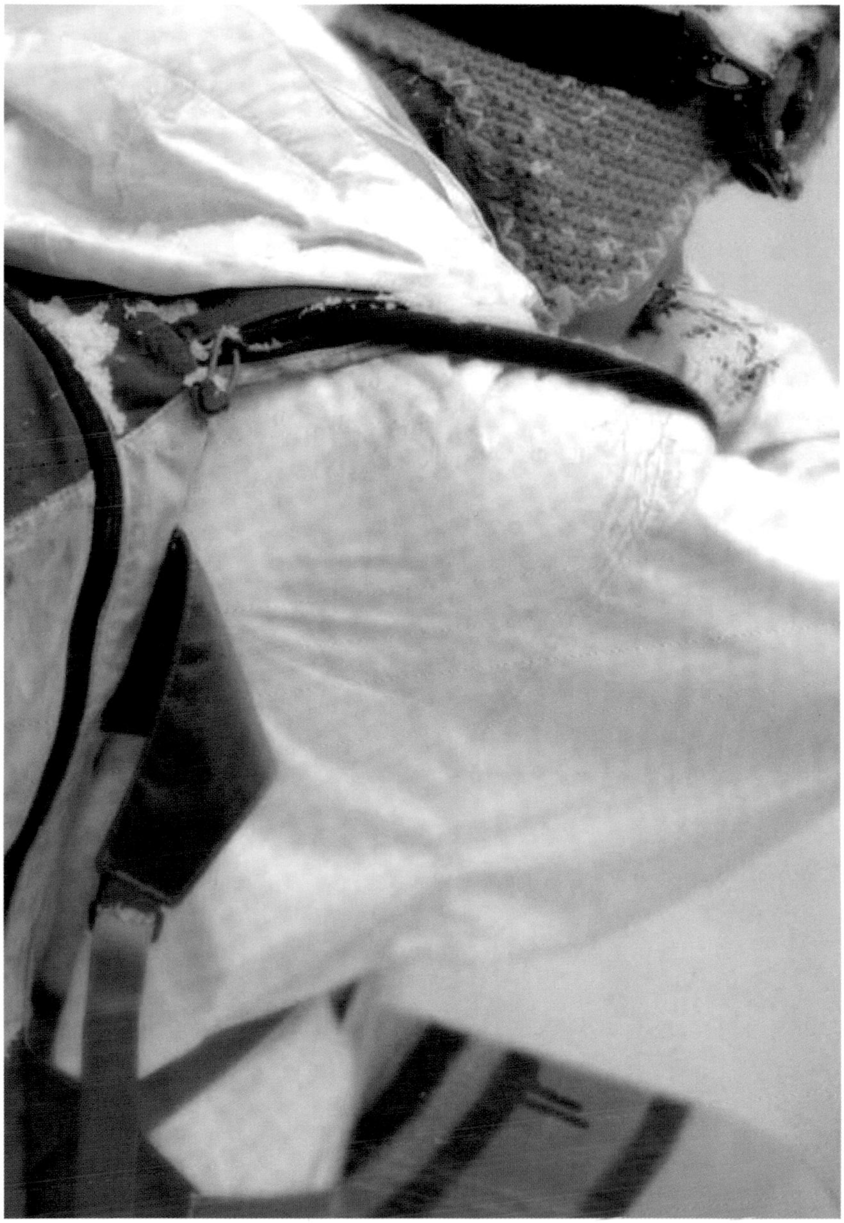

Launched in 2006, Draftfcb is a modern agency model for clients seeking creative, accountable marketing programs that build business and deliver a high Return on Ideas TM. With more than 130 years of combined expertise, the company has its roots in both consumer advertising and behavioral, data-driven direct marketing. The agency is the first global, behavior-based, fully inclusive, highly creative and accountable marketing communications organization to operate against a single P&L. The Draftfcb network spans 110 countries, with more than 9,000 employees worldwide, and is part of the Interpublic Group of Companies (NYSE: IPG). The agency's global corporate leadership team includes Howard Draft, chairman and CEO, Laurence Boschetto, president and COO, Jonathan Harries, worldwide chief creative officer, and Neil Miller, CFO. For more information, visit www.draftfcb.com.

Creada en 2006, Draftfcb es un modelo de agencia moderna para clientes que buscan programas de marketing modernos y responsables que consolidan negocios y consiguen grandes ganancias con sus ideas. Con más de 130 años de experiencia combinada, la empresa tiene sus raíces tanto en publicidad de consumo como en marketing directo centrado en el comportamiento y los datos. La agencia es la primera organización de comunicación y marketing global, basada en el comportamiento, integral, altamente creativa y responsable que opera contra una única cuenta de resultados (P&L). La red de Draftfcb se extiende en 110 países, con más de 9.000 empleados en todo el mundo, y forma parte del Interpublic Group of Companies (NYSE: IPG). El equipo de gestión corporativa incluye a Howard Draft, presidente de la junta directiva y director general, Laurence Boschetto, presidente y director ejecutivo de operaciones, Jonathan Harries, director creativo internacional, y Neil Miller, director de finanzas. Para más información, visite www.draftfcb.com.

Campaing: Stupid situations Client: Camelbak Australia

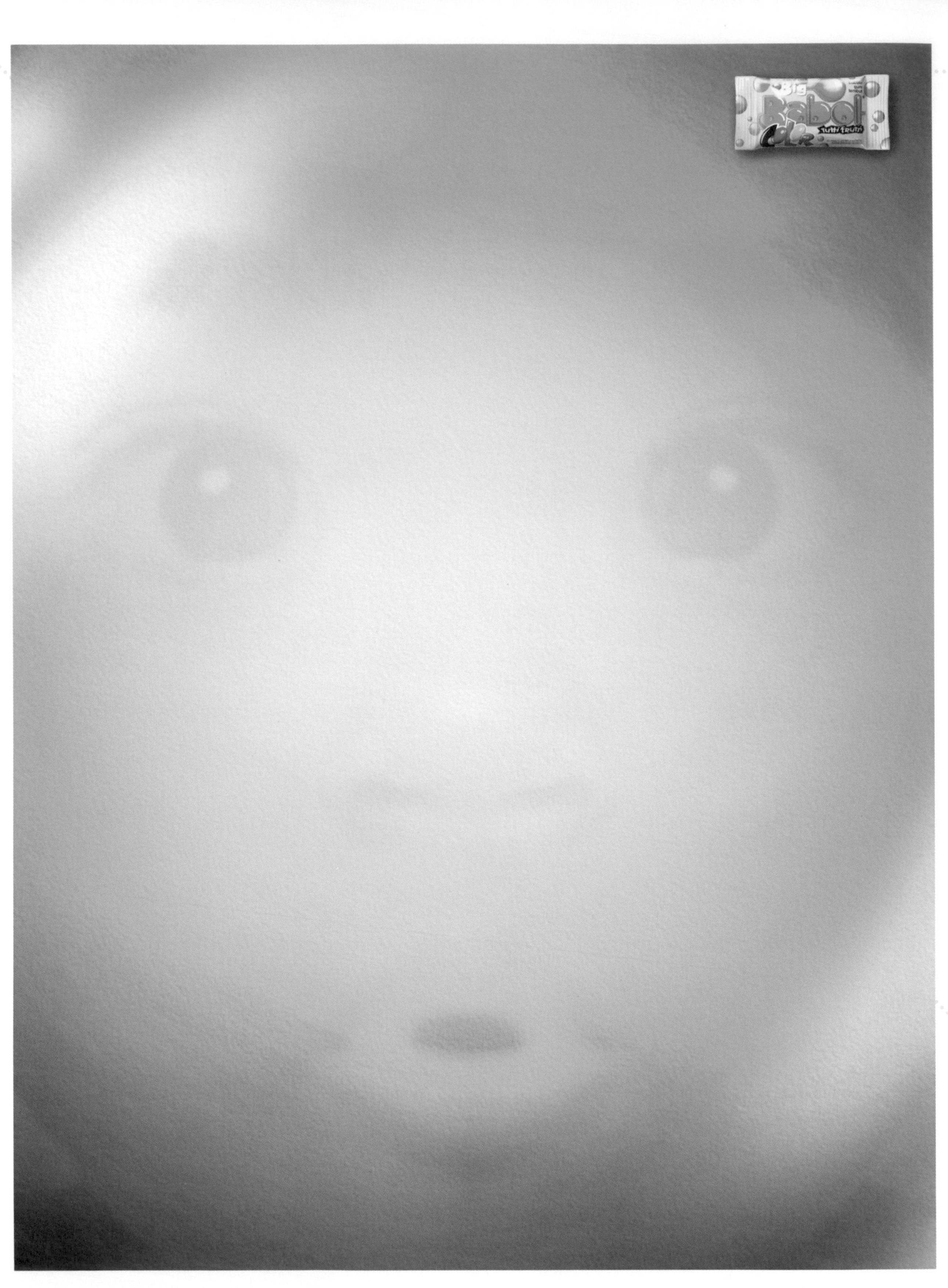
Big
Babol
tutti frutti

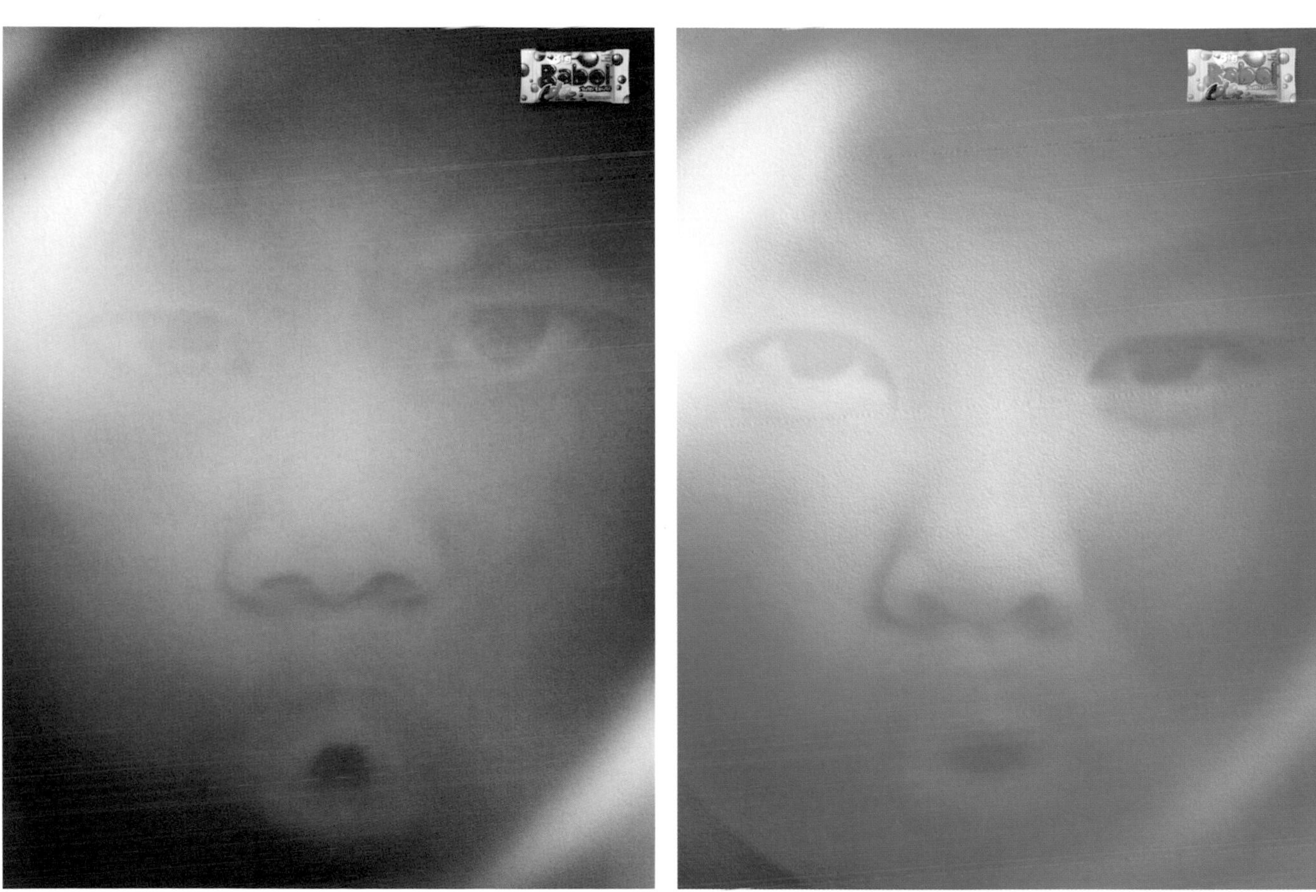

Campaing: Color Client: Big Babol

Campaing: Stupid situations Client: Camelbak Australia

Camelbak Hands-Free Hydration Systems provide water to athletes and adventurers who are just a little too preoccupied to deal with a water bottle. Research shows that the added confidence of knowing they're well stocked with water makes these types more likely to push boundaries they otherwise wouldn't. This press and poster campaign appeals to the hardcore aspirations of all outdoor enthusiasts with a edgy mix of drama and humour. Under the campaign thought of "Designed to endure any situation you're stupid enough to get yourself into", these ads confirm Camelbak's authentic, genuine, category-leader status by aligning the toughness of the product with the very people who use it. Quick run through the desert, anyone?

Camelbak Hands-Free Hydration Systems suministra agua a atletas y aventureros que no quieren cargar con una botella de agua. Un estudio muestra que el hecho de saber que están bien provistos de agua da confianza a los atletas y les ayuda a forzar los límites. Esta campaña de prensa y posters atrae a los entusiastas del deporte al aire libre con una mezcla provocativa de drama y humor. Estos anuncios de la campaña, pensada en términos de "Diseñados para soportar cualquier situación en la que seas lo suficientemente estúpido como para meterse", confirman el estado de auténtico y genuino líder de la categoría de Camelbak, equiparando la resistencia del producto con la resistencia de la gente que lo utiliza. ¿A alguien le apetece venir a correr por el desierto?

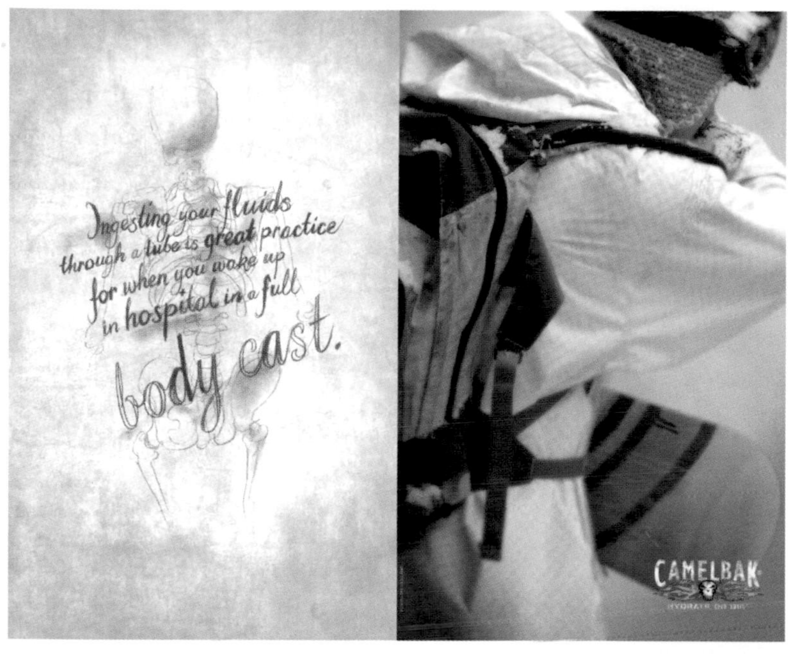
Ingesting your fluids
through a tube is great practice
for when you wake up
in hospital in a full
body cast.
CAMELBAK
HYDRATE OR DIE

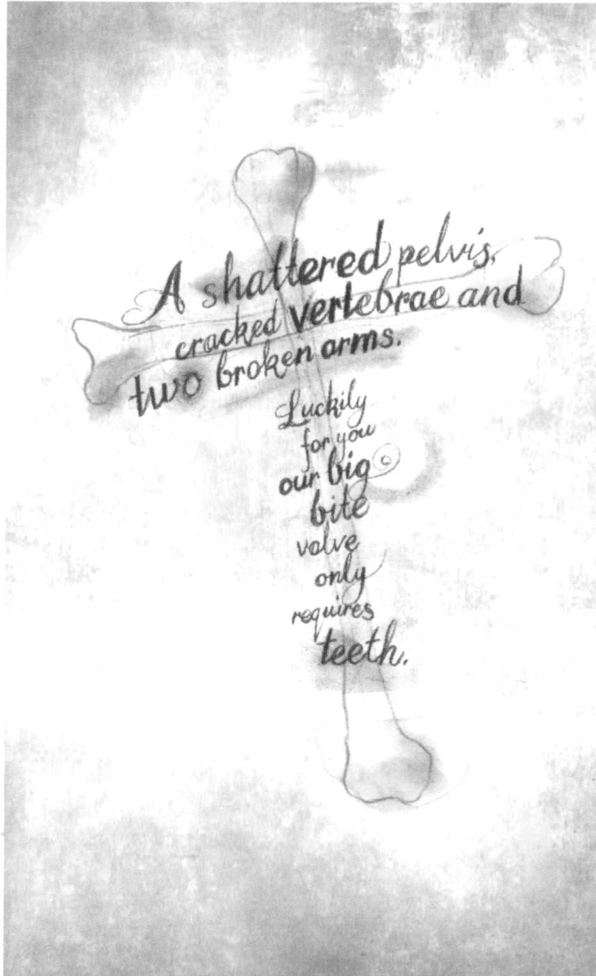
A shattered pelvis,
cracked vertebrae and
two broken arms.
Luckily
for you
our big
bite
valve
only
requires
teeth.

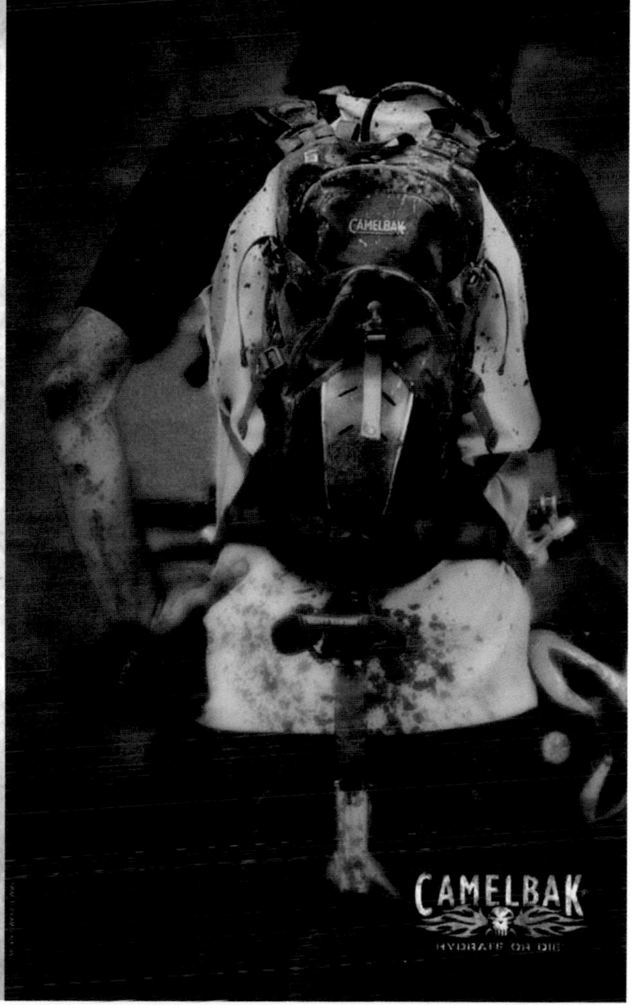
CAMELBAK
CAMELBAK
HYDRATE OR DIE

21
Hu
HUMAN
7E+09
Dow
THE BOND BETWEEN US ALL. It's what we see in each other's eyes. It's how we think about the world around us. It's why, when we read a story about someone we've never met, we feel what they feel. It's a way of seeing that gives us a way of touching. Issues. Ambitions. Lives. It is the Human Element. And that's what The Dow Chemical Company is all about.

76
Hu
HUMAN
7E+09
Dow
HE IS THE BOND BETWEEN CHEMISTRY AND HUMANITY
He is the Human Element. And he is one of the reasons we look at the world a little differently.
Through the eyes of the Human Element

52
Hu
HUMAN
7E+09
Dow

Campaing: Dow Client: The Human Element

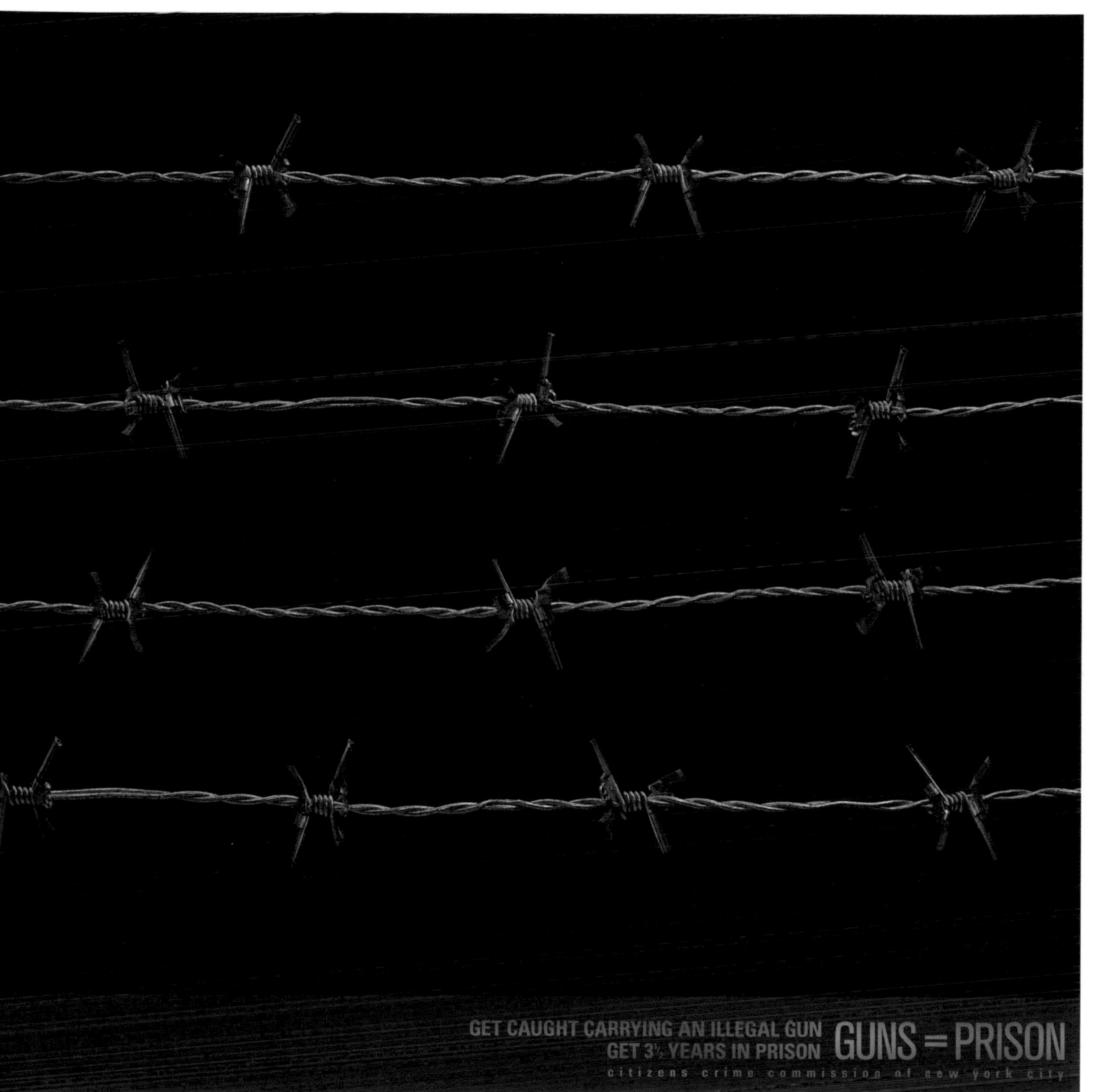
GET CAUGHT CARRYING AN ILLEGAL GUN
GET 3½ YEARS IN PRISON
GUNS = PRISON
citizens crime commission of new york city

Campaing: Citizens Crime Commissionof New York City Client: Guns=Prison

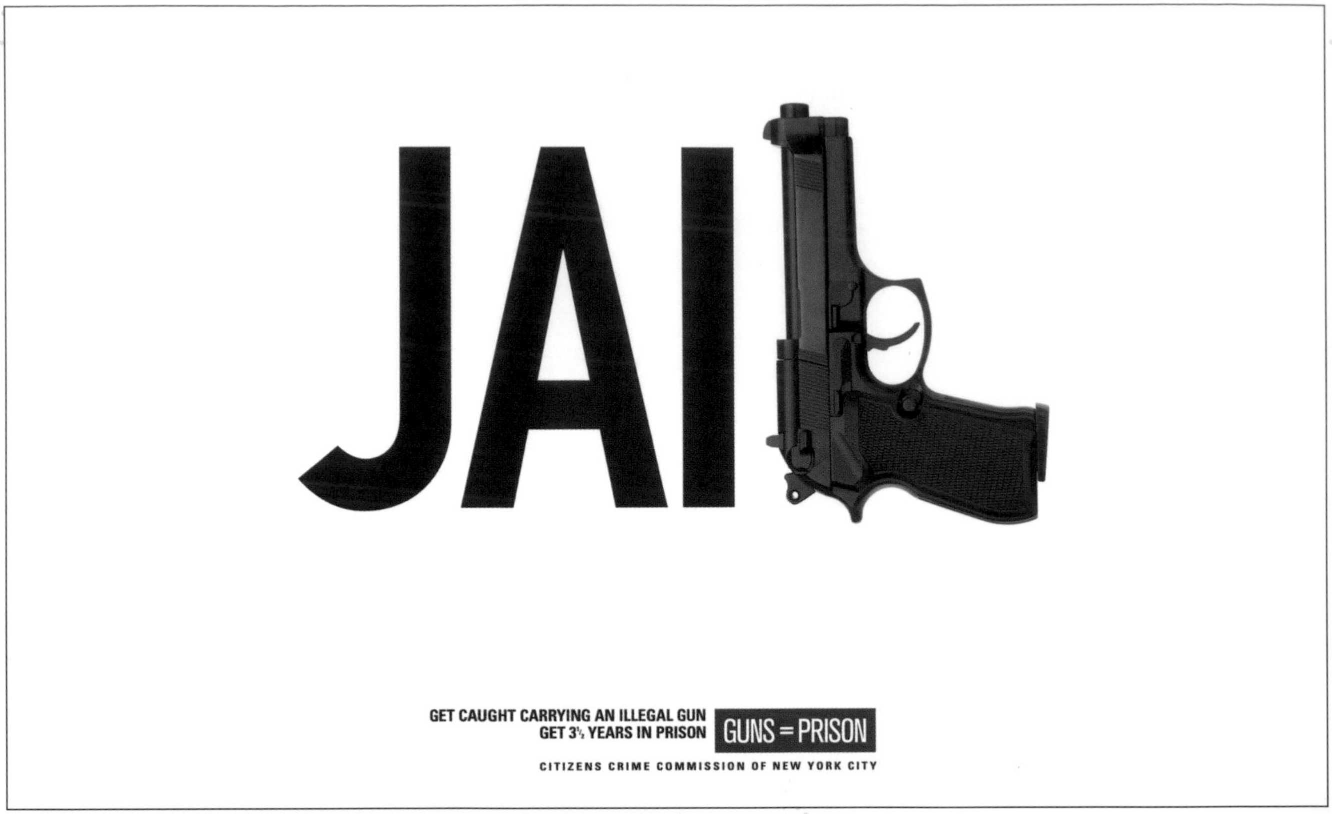

GET CAUGHT CARRYING AN ILLEGAL GUN
GET 3½ YEARS IN PRISON
GUNS = PRISON
CITIZENS CRIME COMMISSION OF NEW YORK CITY

WE WANT ALL ILLEGAL GUNS OUT OF NEW YORK CITY
GET CAUGHT CARRYING AN ILLEGAL GUN
GET 3½ YEARS IN PRISON
GUNS = PRISON
citizens crime commission of new york city

Campaing: Citizens Crime Commissionof New York City Client: Guns=Prison

1:00 pm

3:00 pm

5:00 pm

A specially designed awning placed above the board created a shadow that changed throughout the course of the day.

Campaing: Climate Change Client: World Wildlife Fund

Ignoring global warming won't make it go away.

saveour**climate**.ca

Campaing: Climate Change Client: World Wildlife Fund

According to repeated nationwide surveys...

More Doctors smoke LINCOLNS than any other cigarette!

Not long from now, the way we've been treating the planet will seem just as wrong.

Now that we know better, let's live better. Find out how WWF-Canada can help at **wwf.ca**

Fo… the brand of cigarette preferred by many for its rich flavour. However, did you know that Lincoln is the brand preferred by more Doctors as well? It's true! The secret to their bold taste comes from only using the finest - more expensive Turkish tobacco, as well as our patented curing process. Try them and you'll agree!

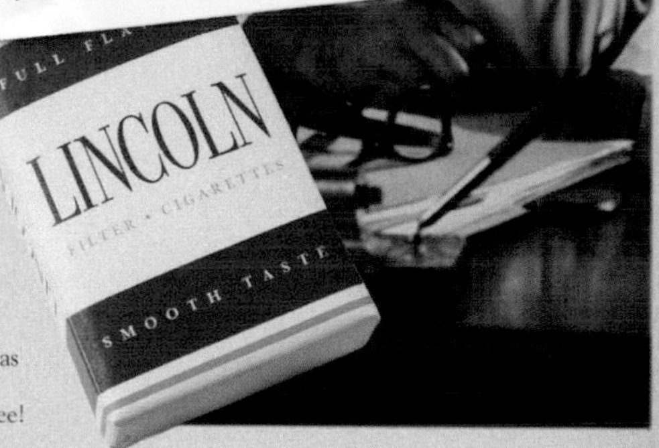

Switch to Lincoln and you'll agree: it's the prescription for flavour!

Campaing: Climate Change Client: World Wildlife Fund

Introducing th

suggested retail: $5,335.00

us Oseo. For a dealer near you visit titusti.com. TITUS

TDA

advertising and design

TDA advertising & design is a relatively happy place, certainly as far as agencies go. We hire good people and work for good clients. We do our best to enjoy the sometimes overwhelming process of creating communication that makes people want to spend their time and money. We have made some mistakes but we have had a substantial impact for a good number of companies and that brings us considerable joy. Come visit us in Boulder, Colorado where our refrigerator has a variety of beer or at tdaad.com. Thanks.

TDA advertising & design es un lugar relativamente feliz, sin duda por lo que respecta a las agencias. Contratamos a buena gente y trabajamos para buenos clientes. Hacemos lo posible por disfrutar del proceso creativo de comunicación, a veces abrumador, que hace que la gente quiera gastar su tiempo y su dinero. Hemos cometido algunos errores, pero hemos conseguido crear un impacto importante para un buen número de empresas y esto nos llena de felicidad. Venga a visitarnos en Boulder (Colorado), donde nuestra nevera contiene una gran variedad de cerveza o en tdaad.com. Gracias.

road trip
THULE
SWEDEN
before you start driving, visit thuleroadtrip.com

Campaing: Roadtrip Client: Thule

So many great stories focus on the open road, and here was our chance to celebrate all of them, even those moments involving flatulence. The campaign was meant to encourage people to take more road trips, as well as remind them how Thule Car Rack Systems can be a part of their next weekend trip, whatever the destination may be. Aside from print, the campaign extends into outdoor, online and viral mediums. For the online segment of the campaign, we pay tribute to "Oregon Trail," a computer game many of us played in elementary school. Thule Trail parodies the journey west in a turbo station wagon, instead of a covered wagon, with a new twist on the obstacles along the way.

Hay muchas historias maravillosas centradas en la carretera, y ésta era nuestra oportunidad para celebrarlas todas, incluso esos momentos que incluyen flatulencias. Con esta campaña queríamos animar a la gente a hacer más viajes por carretera, y recordarles que Thule Car Rack Systems puede ser parte de su siguiente salida de fin de semana, sea cual fuere el destino. La campaña se lanzó en varios medios: impresión, exterior, online, etc. En el segmento online de la campaña, rendimos tributo al juego de ordenador al que la mayoría de nosotros jugábamos cuando íbamos a la escuela, "Oregon Trail". "Thule Trail" imita el viaje al oeste pero en una ranchera turbo en lugar de una carreta cubierta, con nuevos obstáculos por el camino.

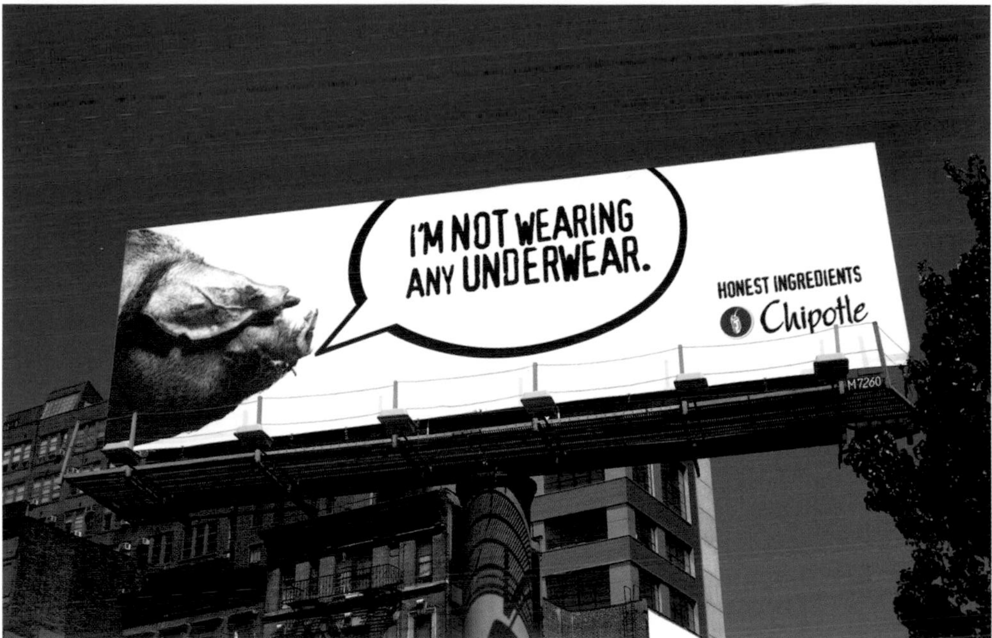

Campaing: Big Burritos Client: Chipotle

La pena de muerte es una práctica de otra época.
Todavía hay 76 países que la aplican.
Amnistía Internacional

CONTRAPUNTO

QUE NINGÚN PAÍS TORURE EN TU NOMBRE.
Amnistía Internacional

Campaing: Banderas Client: Amnistía Internacional

Campaing: Lapidación Client: Amnistía Internacional

CONTRAPUNTO was originally set up in 1974. Now with company offices in Madrid, Barcelona and Alicante, around 150 employees. It is considered to be one of the most creative agencies and the biggest award winner in Spanish history. Amongst the agency's clients we come across such as: Altadis, Amnistía Internacional, As, Barclays Bank, Central Lechera Asturiana, ClickAir, Clickseguros, La Cocinera, Digital+, Google, Groupama, Grupo Chrysler, Jazztel, Jijona, La Rioja Turismo, MercedesBenz, Puma, Reckitt Benckiser, Sanex, Toys R Us and WWF/ADENA.

Actually the Spanish agency to receive most awards in 2006 and 2007.

CONTRAPUNTO fue fundada en 1974. Hoy cuenta con oficinas en Madrid, Barcelona y Alicante y tiene alrededor de 150 empleados. Está considerada como una de las agencias más creativas y es la más premiada en la historia de España. Entre sus clientes se encuentran algunos como: Altadis, Amnistía Internacional, As, Barclays Bank, Central Lechera Asturiana, ClickAir, Clickseguros, La Cocinera, Digital+, Google, Groupama, Grupo Chrysler, Jazztel, Jijona, La Rioja Turismo, MercedesBenz, Puma, Reckitt Benckiser, Sanex, Toys R Us ó WWF/ADENA.

Es la agencia española más premiada en 2006 y 2007.

ena de muerte es una práctica de otra época.
Todavía hay 76 países que la aplican.
Amnistía
Internacional

Campaing: Fusilamiento Client: Amnistía Internacional

QUE NINGÚN PAÍS TORURE EN TU NOMBRE.
Amnistía
Internacional

QUE NINGÚN PAÍS TORURE EN TU NOMBRE.
Amnistía
Internacional

Campaing: Banderas Client: Amnistía Internacional

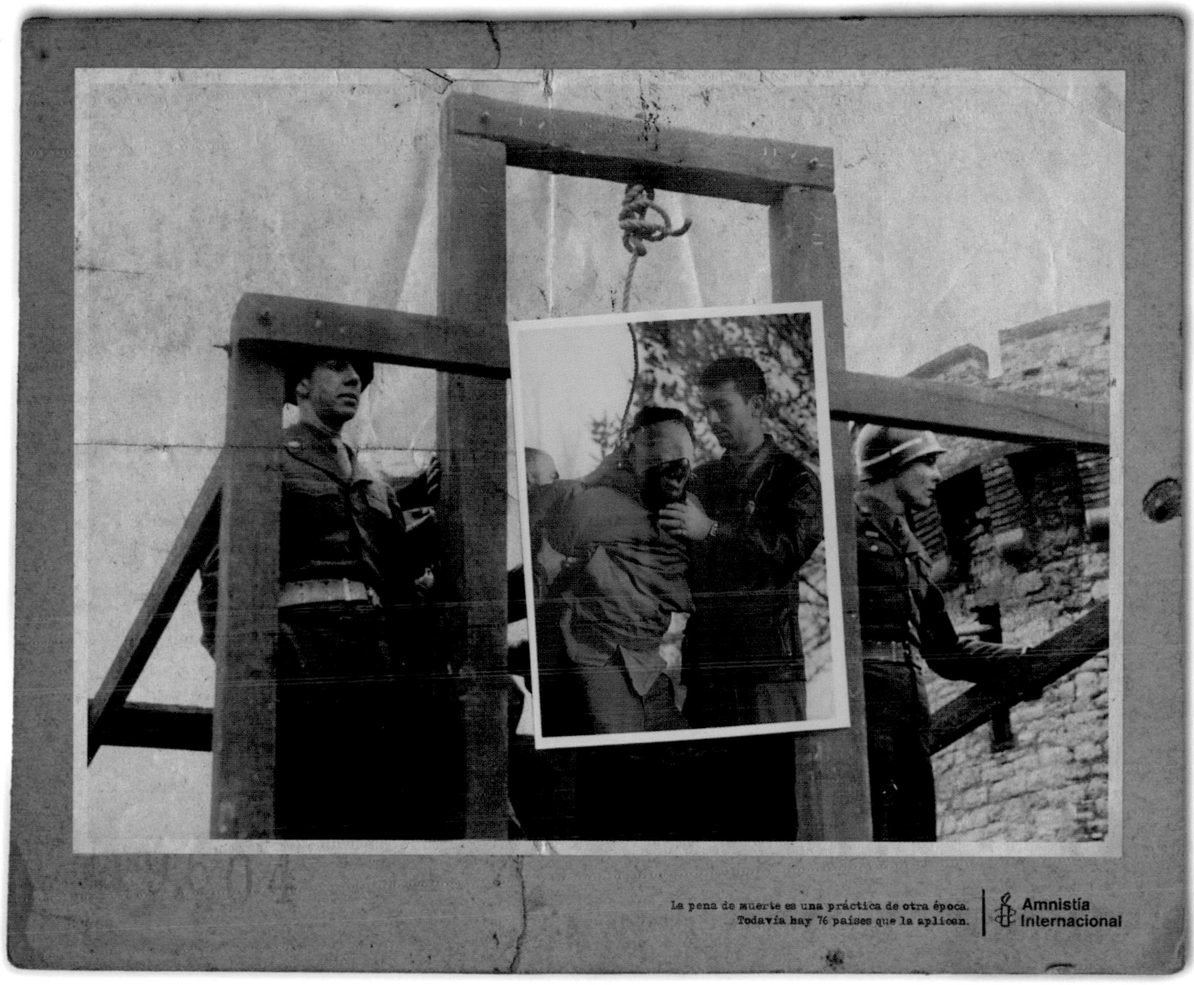

La pena de muerte es una práctica de otra época.
Todavía hay 76 países que la aplican.
Amnistía Internacional

Campaing: Ahorcamiento Client: Amnistía Internacional

Contrapunto, since it began has been noted for its high level of social sensibility becoming involved with various social causes. In 2005 they created CONTRAPUNTOSOCIAL to structure and make a commitment to this will. This brought us closer to one of the biggest assets of communication: to raise awareness and change attitudes to make us more human and provide aid to those less fortunate than ourselves. These projects improve our creative reputation through the success and fame of these campaigns and above all here we are proud to work personally and professionally.

Contrapunto, desde su fundación se ha caracterizado por una alta sensibilidad social involucrándose con distintas causas sociales. En 2005 se creó la marca CONTRAPUNTOSOCIAL que estructura y da forma y compromiso a esta voluntad. Ello nos acerca a uno de los valores esenciales que tiene la comunicación: concienciar y cambiar actitudes que nos hagan más humanos y ayudando a colectivos desfavorecidos. Estos trabajos mejoran nuestra reputación creativa por el éxito y notoriedad de estas campañas y sobre todo, nos enorgullece a los que aquí trabajamos personal y profesionalmente.

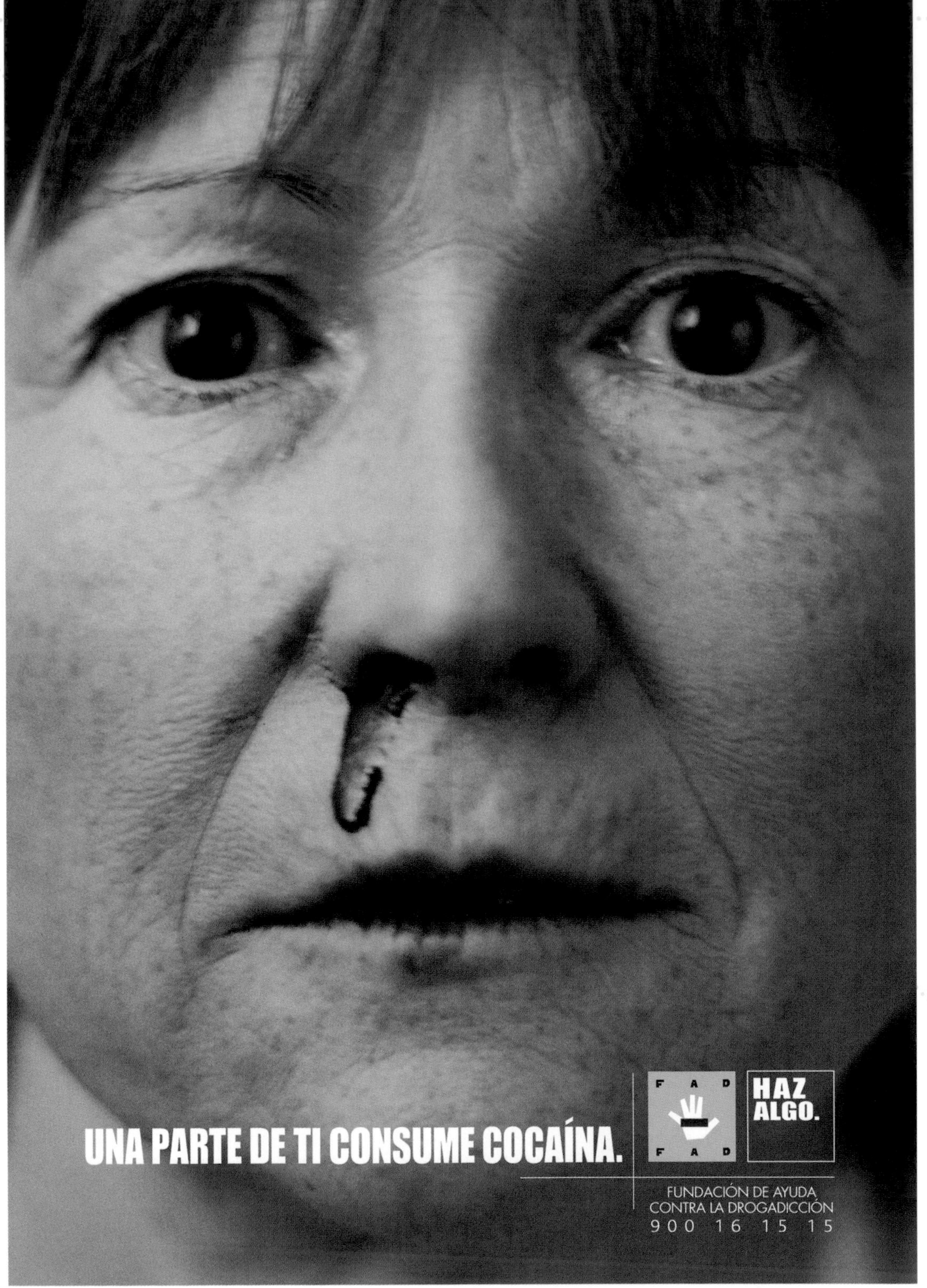

UNA PARTE DE TI CONSUME COCAÍNA.
F A D
F A D
HAZ ALGO.
FUNDACIÓN DE AYUDA CONTRA LA DROGADICCIÓN
900 16 15 15

Campaing: Una parte de ti consume cocaína Client: Fundación de ayuda contra la dogradicción

Campaing: Contaminación Client: WWF

CONTRAPUNTO has now been working for some years on combined solutions for effective communication. The main inspiration for the campaign is CREATIVE INTELLIGENCE, whereby the key is to understand the client's business and to discuss with them the problems which might arise and the possible solutions in the different areas and disciplines across the communication's world.

CONTRAPUNTO has devised a working method known as the "Strategic Board" where, seated alongside those in charge of the brand and communication for the advertiser, are the professionals in research, strategic planning, media, interactive, alternative communication and direct marketing, creativity and corporate identity. The creative idea, the thinking and the idea for the campaign is only sought after each one of the professionals has worked out the solutions specific to their field of work.

CONTRAPUNTO viene trabajando en soluciones integrales de comunicación eficaz desde hace ya varios años. El principio que inspira la compañía es la INTELIGENCIA CREATIVA, donde la clave es entender el negocio de los clientes y compartir con ellos los problemas y las posibles soluciones en las distintas áreas y disciplinas que abarca el ámbito de la comunicación.

CONTRAPUNTO ha creado una metodología de trabajo que llama "Mesa Estratégica" en la que junto a los responsables de marca y comunicación del anunciante se sientan profesionales expertos en investigación, planificación estratégica, medios, interactivo, comunicación alternativa y marketing directo, creatividad e identidad corporativa. Se busca, antes de la idea creativa, el pensamiento y la idea de la campaña y sólo después cada uno de los profesionales desarrolla las soluciones especificas de su área de trabajo.

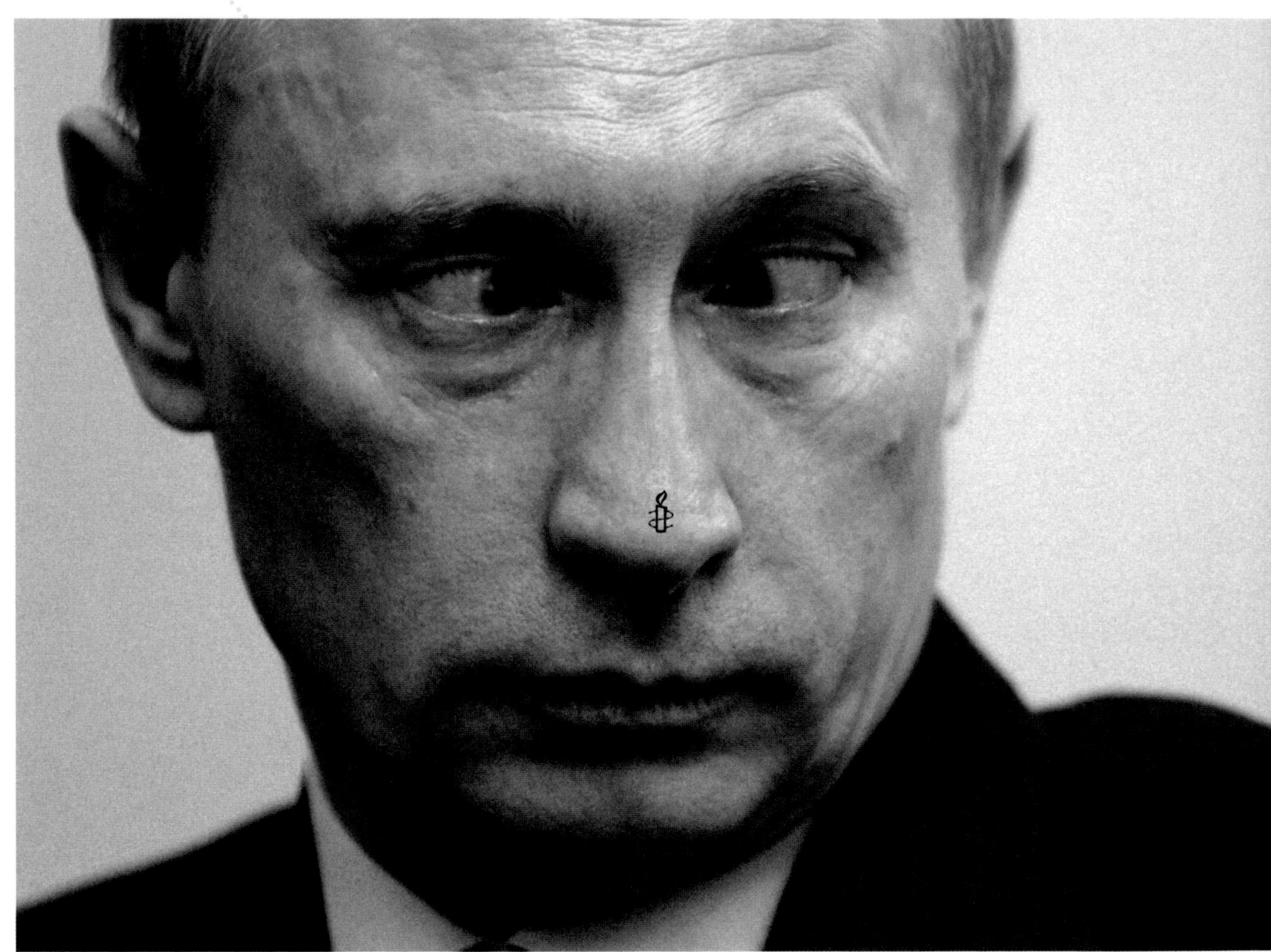

Campaing: Mosca Client: Amnistía Internacional

fafi
BONER CITY!!
Harmony PAPER TOWEL

ALT TERRAIN

ALT TERRAIN's founder, Adam Salacuse, raised in raised in Brooklyn, New York, took all he learned about people, culture, and street credibility and applied them to the world of advertising. He took note that radio ads, TV commercials, and outdoor billboards had a minimal effect on his or his friends' choices in clothes, cars, foods, music and other lifestyle preferences. Friends, family, but more importantly the power of metro market street culture (e.g. diversity, music, street trends, DJs, graffiti artists, Hip-Hop, city sports, etc.) seemed to have the most impact on consumer product choices around him. He enter the advertising industry in 1999 with an idea to create advertising media that has a function (such as coffee cup sleeve ads), to offerings that people enjoy and embrace (such as public space brand installations), and most recently the focus is on advertising media that makes a positive impact on people and society.

El fundador de ALT TERRAIN, Adam Salacuse, es de Brooklyn (Nueva York). Cogió todo lo que había aprendido sobre la gente, la cultura y la calle y lo aplicó al mundo de la publicidad. Se fijó en que los anuncios de radio, de televisión, y los carteles publicitarios prácticamente no influían en su elección o la de sus amigos de ropa, coches, comidas, música, etc. Los amigos, la familia y sobre todo la cultura callejera metropolitana (la diversidad, la música, las tendencias callejeras, los DJs, los artistas de graffiti, el Hip-Hop, los deportes urbanos, etc.) parecían ser lo que más influía en las elecciones de productos en su entorno. Entró en la industria de la publicidad en 1999 con la idea de crear un medio publicitario que tuviera una función (como por ejemplo anuncios en los manguitos de protección de los vasos de café) y productos que la gente disfrutara y adoptara (como instalaciones de marcas en espacios públicos). Más recientemente se centra en medios publicitarios que tengan un impacto positivo en la gente y en la sociedad.

Campaing: Helio Client: Helio

Campaing: Disney Client: Disney

New Art Center

NEW ART CENTER
61 Washington Park
Newtonville, MA 02460
tel: (617) 964-3424
www.newartcenter.org

Non-Profit Org.
U.S. Postage
PAID
Newton, MA 02460
Permit #55312

SPOTHUNTERS.

THE FINE ART OF REAL ESTATE.

Shepard Fairey www.obeygiant.com
Greg Lamarche SPOTHUNTERS logo
Caleb Neelon www.theartwheredreamscometrue.com
Monster Project www.cantabpublishing.com

The SPOTHUNTERS artists each use galleries, city streets, and publishing as venues. Come see why.

March 6 – April 7, 2006
Opening Reception: Friday, March 10, 6-9 pm.
Film Screening: "Andre the Giant Has a Posse" and other surprises: Thursday, March 16, 7pm.
Gallery talk with Caleb Neelon: Sunday, March 26, 2pm.
Holzwasser Gallery: works by Jocelyn Chemel
Gallery hours: Monday – Friday, 9-5; Sunday 1-5; closed on Saturdays.

ASL interpreter available upon request.

kidrobot presents...

TURBO LOVER
NEW PAINTINGS BY
BUFF MONSTER

April 20–May 30, 2006
Opening Reception April 20, 6-8 pm
@ Kidrobot LA

Customer Inquiries: sales@kidrobot.com
Press Inquiries: press@kidrobot.com
Phone: 310-576-7766

HELIO

buffmonster.com

KIDROBOT LA 1407 3rd STREET PROMENADE, SANTA MONICA www.kidrobot.com

Campaing: Helio Client: Helio

Helio, a new entrant in the highly competitive mobile phone industry in the United States desired to connect their brand with trend-setting, affluent consumers. "StreetVirus", the creative agency, crafted a brand campaign to attract and engage the gatekeepers of street culture; namely contemporary artists and retail establishments frequented by trend-setting consumers.

Instead of a heavy-handed approach, Helio sponsored two contemporary artists in San Francisco, New York City, Los Angeles, Boston, and Chicago providing them with high-profile wall space to paint murals to their liking, plus assisted with their art local shows. Artists incorporated the Helio flame logo into their murals in a manner which complemented their art. Furthermore, artists thanked Helio by recognizing them on gallery show invitations and interior branding.

"StreetVirus" offered trend-setting retail establishments (e.g. hair salons, clothing boutiques, skate/surf shops, etc.) the opportunity to host a Helio Lounge where consumers could preview the phones before they were available to the public, plus supplied the owners and store staff with complimentary Helio phones.

The participatory influencer outreach initiative endeared trend-spreading artists and establishments, plus set the stage for the official launch of the brand which resulted in +100,000 new subscribers within the first year.

Helio, un nuevo integrante de la altamente competitiva industria de la telefonía móvil en Estados Unidos, deseaba conectar su marca con consumidores acaudalados y marcadores de tendencias. La agencia creativa "StreetVirus", ideó una campaña para atraer a los guardianes de la cultura callejera, principalmente artistas contemporáneos y comercios minoristas frecuentados por consumidores que marcan tendencias.

En lugar de un enfoque severo, Helio patrocinó a dos artistas contemporáneos en San Francisco, Nueva York, Los Angeles, Boston, y Chicago proporcionándoles paredes en lugares destacados para que pintaran murales a su gusto. Los artistas incorporaron el logotipo de Helio en sus murales de modo que complementara su arte. Además, los artistas se lo agradecieron a Helio mencionándolos en invitaciones a exposiciones en galerías y desarrollando la marca en interiores.

"StreetVirus" le ofreció a los comercios que marcan tendencias (como peluquerías, tiendas de ropa, tiendas de skate/surf, etc.) la oportunidad de presentar un Helio Lounge donde los consumidores pudieran ver los teléfonos antes de que salieran a la venta para el público, y además les proporcionó teléfonos Helio complementarlos a los propietarios y a los trabajadores de las tiendas.

Esta iniciativa encantó a artistas y establecimientos de vanguardia, y además creó el marco para el lanzamiento oficial de la marca que resultó en más de 100.000 nuevos suscritores en el primer año.

Campaing: Giant Shoe Client: Onitsuka Tiger

strawberry frog

Founded on Valentine's Day 1999, by chief executive Brian Elliott, StrawberryFrog Amsterdam is an award-winning full-service international communications agency based in Holland.

Since launch StrawberryFrog has sparked cultural movements for the world's most respected brands including ASICS Onitsuka Tiger, Chevrolet, Coca Cola, Heineken, IKEA, Mitsubishi, Opel, Sony Ericsson and Panasonic.

StrawberryFrog's multi-cultural strategic, creative, digital, media and management teams work in collaboration with clients to create highly effective and integrated pan European and global campaigns. For more than eight years, it has built passionate customer relationships and delivered results for clients who think big.

Fundada en el día de San Valentín de 1999 por el Director General Brian Elliott, StrawberryFrog Amsterdam es una galardonada agencia de comunicación integral ubicada en Holanda.

Desde su lanzamiento, StrawberryFrog ha desencadenado movimientos culturales para algunas de las marcas más respetadas del mundo como ASICS Onitsuka Tiger, Chevrolet, Coca Cola, Heineken, IKEA, Mitsubishi, Opel, Sony Ericsson y Panasonic.

Los equipos estratégicos, creativos, digitales, de medios y de gestión de StrawberryFrog trabajan en colaboración con los clientes para crear campañas paneuropeas y globales altamente efectivas. Durante más de ocho años, ha construido apasionadas relaciones con los clientes y ha obtenido grandes resultados para clientes que piensan en grande.

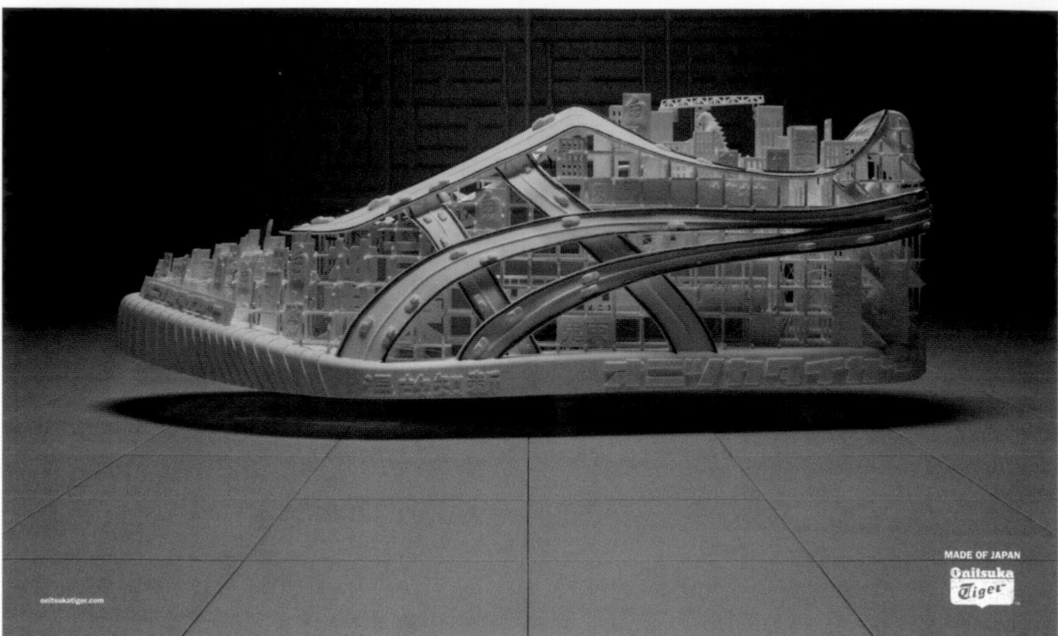

Campaing: Electric Shoe_Off Client: Onitsuka Tiger

The objective was to build on the global strategy of Made of Japan and go beyond traditional advertising to create a culturally authentic integrated campaign that impacts across all media touchpoints. Key were print and online media to support physical installations to be displayed in Onitsuka Tiger stores and key retail outlets worldwide.

The installations include 1 meter, 70cm and 40cm sculptures, supported by two 30-second films (animation/TVC and a 'making of'). There is point of sale (postcard and shoe displays), magazine and newspaper print adverts, window stickers, luminous USB sticks, keyrings and a typeface. There are also internet virals and banner adverts.

The "Electric Light Shoe" sculpture pays homage to the city of Tokyo in miniature. It is filled with sweeping miniature highways packed with minute Toyotas, and high-rise buildings that form Tokyo's urban skyline. Planes queue-up on a replica Narita Airport runway where the sneaker's tongue should be, there are Japanese market signs in the toe, a vending machine selling miniature Onitsuka Tigers in the heel, and a neon metro train hurtles throughout the shoe.

El objetivo era construir sobre la estrategia global de Made of Japan e ir más allá de la publicidad tradicional para crear una campaña integrada culturalmente que tuviera una repercusión en todos los puntos de contacto de los medios. Los medios impresos y online fueron clave para apoyar las instalaciones físicas que se exhibieron en las tiendas Onitsuka Tiger y en puntos de venta clave.

Las instalaciones incluyen esculturas de 1 metro, de 70 cm., y de 40 cm., acompañadas de dos películas de 30 segundos (animación/TVC y "making of"). Hay un punto de venta (exposición de postales y zapatos), anuncios impresos en revistas y periódicos, pegatinas de ventanas, lápices USB luminosos, llaveros y un tipo de letra. También hay anuncios virales en Internet y banners publicitarios.

La escultura "Electric Light Shoe" rinde tributo a la ciudad de Tokio en miniatura. Está repleta de autopistas en miniatura con diminutos Toyotas, y rascacielos que forman el contorno urbano de Tokio. Los aviones hacen cola en la pista de la réplica del Aeropuerto de Narita, ahí donde debería estar la lengüeta de las zapatillas deportivas; hay signos del mercado japonés en los dedos; una máquina expendedora que vende Onitsuka Tigers en miniatura en el talón y un metro de neón se precipita por el zapato.

温故知新

onitsukatiger.com

MADE OF JAPAN

Onitsuka Tiger

Campaing: Electric Shoe_Off Client: Onitsuka Tiger

NOTICE
I'm in a foul mood and you're all coming with me. Thanks.
–THE ECONOMY

Campaing: Sooth Sayer Client: Cap Gemini Ernst & Young

Campaing: Rooftops Client: Heineken Champions League

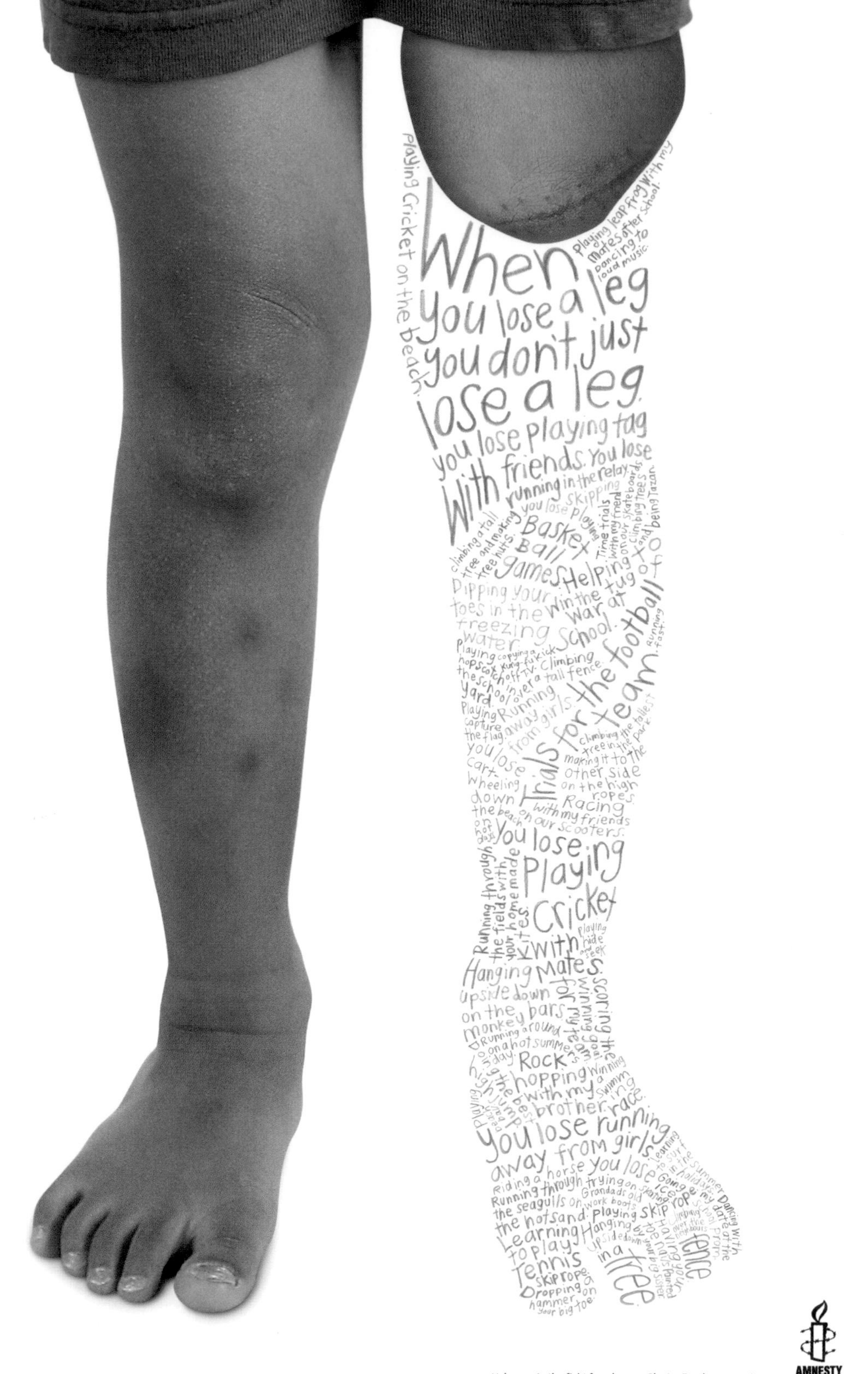
When you lose a leg you don't just lose a leg.
You lose playing tag with friends. You lose
Playing Cricket on the beach.
Trials for the football team.
You lose playing Cricket with mates.
You lose running away from girls.
Help us win the fight for a ban on Cluster Bombs. amnesty.org.nz
AMNESTY INTERNATIONAL

publicis MOJO

Campaing: Candles Client: Amnesty International

Campaing: Lose Client: Amnesty International

Publicis Mojo is a global agency which works on some of the world's greatest brands.
Among its impressive portfolio lies a wonderful mix of local iconic New Zealand brands as well as big international names such as "Diet Coke", "Powerade" and "Schweppes".
Hungry and restless by nature, Publicis Mojo has earned the well deserved reputation for being a key player on the international market –its appointment as global creative agency for "Diet Coke" is testament to this and an achievement the agency is particularly proud of.
Top creative talent together with a determination to know everything humanly possible about the consumer, is what drives Publicis Mojo to produce world class, award winning work that connects with the target audience everytime.

Publicis Mojo es una agencia global que trabaja con algunas de las mejores marcas del mundo. Su impresionante cartera está formada por varias marcas icónicas neozelandesas y destacados nombres internacionales como "Diet Coke", "Powerade" y "Schweppes".
Hambrienta e inquieta por naturaleza, la agencia Publicis Mojo se ha ganado la fama bien merecida de ser un jugador clave en el mercado internacional. Su nombramiento como agencia creativa global para "Diet Coke" es testimonio de ello y es un logro del que está particularmente orgullosa.
Un gran talento creativo junto a la determinación para saberlo todo sobre el consumidor, es lo que permite que Publicis Mojo pueda crear publicidad de nivel mundial y galardonada que conecta siempre con la audiencia objetivo.

Campaing: Candles Client: Amnesty International

Every year Amnesty International helps in the release of thousands of prisoners of conscience. The logo of amnesty is famous as an icon of freedom. By placing this logo in real pictures of people in need it appears as if the amnesty candle is burning through their ropes, helping to free them.

Cada año, Amnistía Internacional ayuda a la liberación de miles de prisioneros de conciencia. El logotipo de amnistía es famoso como icono de la libertad. Al colocar este logotipo en fotografías reales de personas necesitadas, parece que la vela de amnistía esté quemando sus cuerdas, ayudando a liberarlas.

Campaing: Candles Client: Amnesty International

Half of the oxygen we breathe comes from our oceans.
Keep our oceans alive.
GREENPEACE
www.greenpeace.org.au

Campaing: Ocean defenders direct campaign Client: GreenPeace

To encourage people to protect our oceans by signing up to become an "Ocean Defender" and communicate that "half the oxygen we breathe comes from our oceans".

Implementation:
Match the movements of the tides with the sound of human breathing to highlight that the oceans produce 50% of our oxygen, and that they are living entities that keep us and our planet alive. The message concludes with a link to a Greenpeace site to recruit "Ocean Defenders".

Results:
125,000 new Ocean Defenders.

Esta campaña pretende animar a la gente a proteger nuestros océanos inscribiéndose como "Defensor del Océano" y comunicar que "la mitad del oxígeno que respiramos viene de los océanos".

Implementación:
Equiparar los movimientos de las mareas con la respiración humana para subrayar que los océanos producen el 50% de nuestro oxígeno, y que son entes vivos que nos mantienen a nosotros y a nuestro planeta en vida. El mensaje concluye con un link a la página de Greenpeace para reclutar "Defensores del Océano".

Resultados:
125.000 nuevos Defensores del Oceano.

KEEP IT SAFE, KEEP IT HIDDEN

PHONES GET THE BEST
RECEPTION OUTSIDE A STATION.

THIEVES EXPECT YOU TO CHECK YOUR PHONE
AS SOON AS YOU GET OUTSIDE.

www.homeoffice.gov.uk

rkcr y&r

You wouldn't allow strangers to watch your child in the real world.
Why allow it in the virtual world?
Using a webcam or emailing photos might seem like innocent fun. As long as you can be certain who's on the receiving end. Talk to your children and tell them not to send images of themselves to people they don't really know. For more advice, visit our website. It's one part of the net that can help your kids safely explore the rest. www.internetsafetyzone.com
Home Office

The virtual world has many of the dangers of the real world.
So why let children explore it by themselves?
Although the internet can be perfectly safe, the young and inexperienced could still end up talking to strangers, encountering pornography, or even being bullied online. For more advice, see our website. It's one part of the net that can help your kids safely explore the rest. www.internetsafetyzone.com
Home Office

Campaing: Child Protection on the Internet Client: Home Office

Campaing: Acquisitive Crime Reduction Client: Home Office

RKCR/Y&R London as it exists today was formed by the merger of Y&R London and RKCR in 1999. RKCR was founded in 1993, and has been trading for the last 14 years. Young & Rubicam was founded in Philadelphia in 1923 when John Orr Young, an Account Executive, and Raymond Rubicam, a copywriter, formed their partnership. Today, the Young & Rubicam brands global network includes more than 182 offices in 82 countries. Y&R brands and in turn RKCR/Y&R became a wholly owned subsidiary of WPP when it was bought by them in 2000.

Top Clients: M&S, Lloyds TSB, Bacardi, Land Rover, Oxfam.

We believe that only brands with the energy to constantly delight their audience with new ideas and innovations will survive, so we're structured in a way that ensures creative energy flows as feely as possible. There are no departments, no gatekeepers between creative teams and clients, and minimal hierarchy.

RKCR/Y&R London, tal como existe hoy se creó gracias a la fusión entre Y&R London y RKCR en 1999. RKCR fue fundada en 1993 y ha estado activa durante los últimos 14 años. Young & Rubicam fue fundada en Filadelfia en 1923 cuando John Orr Young, un ejecutivo de cuentas y Raymond Rubicam, un redactor publicitario, se asociaron. Actualmente, la red global de las marcas Young & Rubicam incluye más de 182 oficinas en 82 países. Las marcas Y&R y RKCR/Y&R se convirtieron en filial propiedad de WPP cuando las adquirió en el año 2000.

Clientes principales: M&S, Lloyds TSB, Bacardi, Land Rover, Oxfam.

Creemos que solo sobrevivirán las empresas que tengan energía suficiente para seducir constantemente a la audiencia con nuevas ideas e innovaciones, por lo que nos estructuramos de modo que la energía creativa fluya lo más libremente posible. No hay departamentos, ni guardianes entre los equipos creativos y los clientes, y la jerarquía es mínima.

Campaing: Alcohol Anti-Social Behavior Reduction Client: Home Office

Campaing: Rape Reduction Client: Home Office

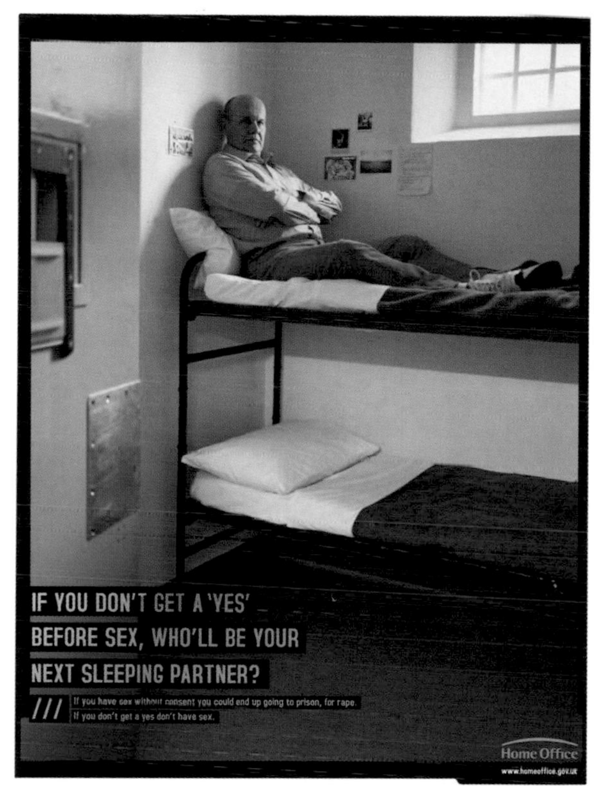

IF YOU DON'T GET A 'YES'
BEFORE SEX, WHO'LL BE YOUR
NEXT SLEEPING PARTNER?
///
If you have sex without consent you could end up going to prison, for rape.
If you don't get a yes don't have sex.
Home Office
www.homeoffice.gov.uk

Campaing: Anti-Kerb Crawling Client: Home Office

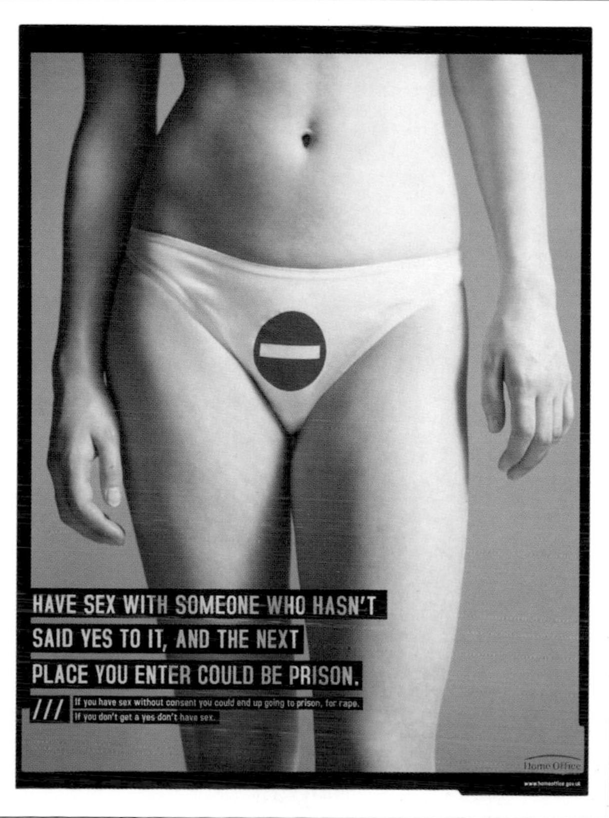

HAVE SEX WITH SOMEONE WHO HASN'T
SAID YES TO IT, AND THE NEXT
PLACE YOU ENTER COULD BE PRISON.
///
If you have sex without consent you could end up going to prison, for rape.
If you don't get a yes don't have sex.
Home Office
www.homeoffice.gov.uk

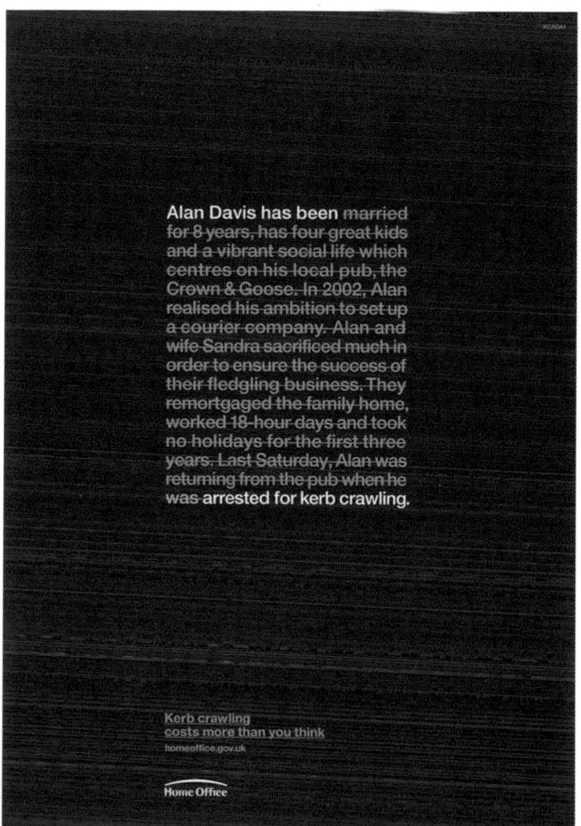

Alan Davis has been married for 8 years, has four great kids and a vibrant social life which centres on his local pub, the Crown & Goose. In 2002, Alan realised his ambition to set up a courier company. Alan and wife Sandra sacrificed much in order to ensure the success of their fledgling business. They remortgaged the family home, worked 18-hour days and took no holidays for the first three years. Last Saturday, Alan was returning from the pub when he was arrested for kerb crawling.
Kerb crawling
costs more than you think
homeoffice.gov.uk
Home Office

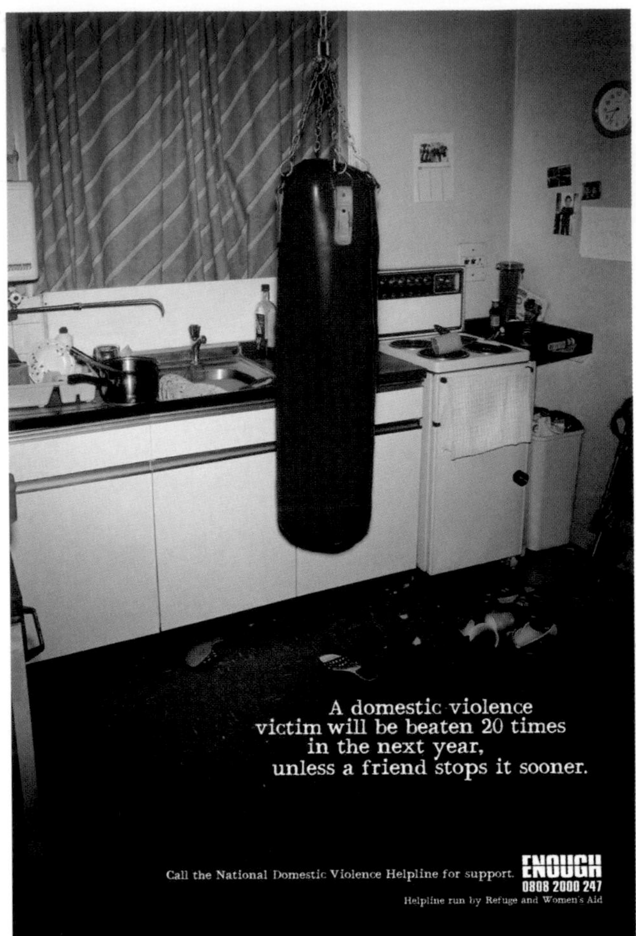

A domestic violence
victim will be beaten 20 times
in the next year,
unless a friend stops it sooner.
Call the National Domestic Violence Helpline for support.
ENOUGH
0808 2000 247
Helpline run by Refuge and Women's Aid

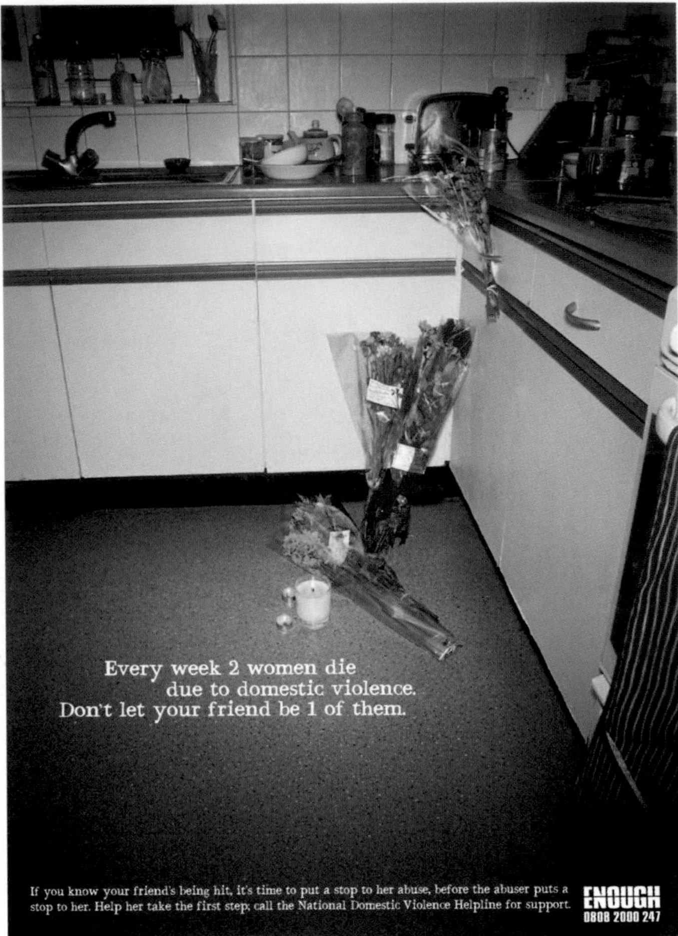

Every week 2 women die
due to domestic violence.
Don't let your friend be 1 of them.
If you know your friend's being hit, it's time to put a stop to her abuse, before the abuser puts a stop to her. Help her take the first step; call the National Domestic Violence Helpline for support.
ENOUGH
0808 2000 247

Campaing: Domestic Violence Reduction Client: Home Office

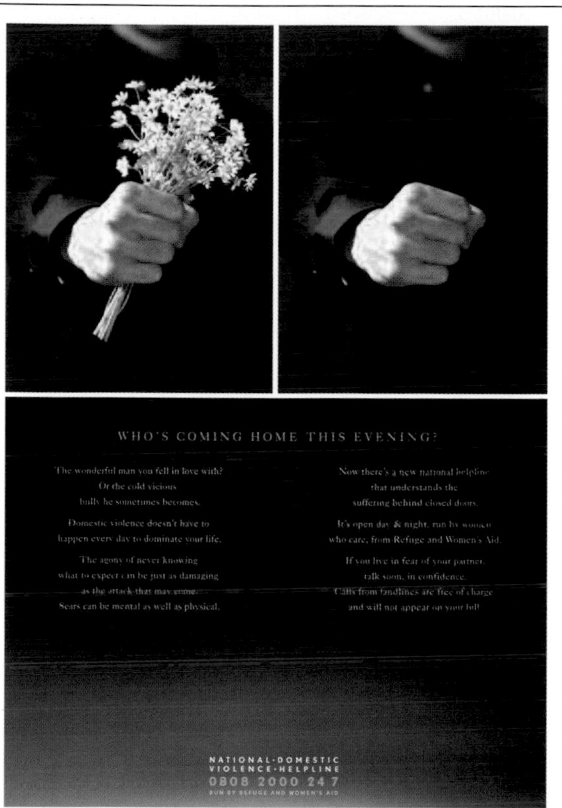

WHO'S COMING HOME THIS EVENING?
The wonderful man you fell in love with?
Or the cold vicious
bully he sometimes becomes.
Domestic violence doesn't have to
happen every day to dominate your life.
The agony of never knowing
what to expect can be just as damaging
as the attack that may come.
Scars can be mental as well as physical.
Now there's a new national helpline
that understands the
suffering behind closed doors.
It's open day & night, run by women
who care, from Refuge and Women's Aid.
If you live in fear of your partner,
talk soon, in confidence.
Calls from landlines are free of charge
and will not appear on your bill
NATIONAL·DOMESTIC
VIOLENCE·HELPLINE
0808 2000 247

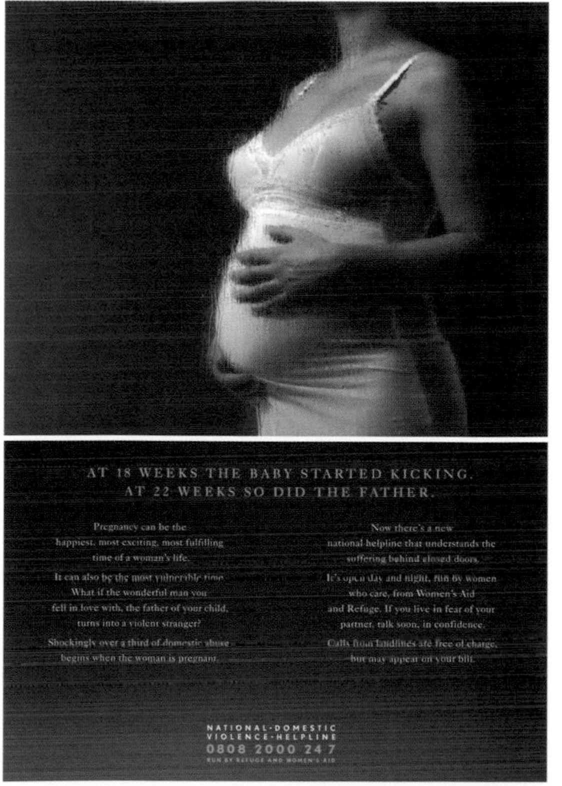

AT 18 WEEKS THE BABY STARTED KICKING.
AT 22 WEEKS SO DID THE FATHER.
Pregnancy can be the
happiest, most exciting, most fulfilling
time of a woman's life.
It can also be the most vulnerable time.
What if the wonderful man you
fell in love with, the father of your child,
turns into a violent stranger?
Shockingly over a third of domestic abuse
begins when the woman is pregnant.
Now there's a new
national helpline that understands the
suffering behind closed doors.
It's open day and night, run by women
who care, from Women's Aid
and Refuge. If you live in fear of your
partner, talk soon, in confidence.
Calls from landlines are free of charge,
but may appear on your bill.
NATIONAL·DOMESTIC
VIOLENCE·HELPLINE
0808 2000 247

Campaing: Domestic Violence Reduction Client: Home Office

[1], [2], [3],
[4], [5], [6],
[7], [8], [9],
[*], [0], [#],

How do u become
a victim of mobile
phone theft?

Buy a stolen mobile.

Stolen mobiles
can now be blocked
within 48hrs.

r u gettin the msg?

Home Office

homeoffice.gov.uk

Campaing: Stolen Mobile Blocking Client: Home Office

When your stolen
mobile stops working
don't worry.
We're sure you'll
get a refund.

Stolen mobiles
can now be blocked
within 48hrs.

r u gettin the msg?

Home Office

homeoffice.gov.uk

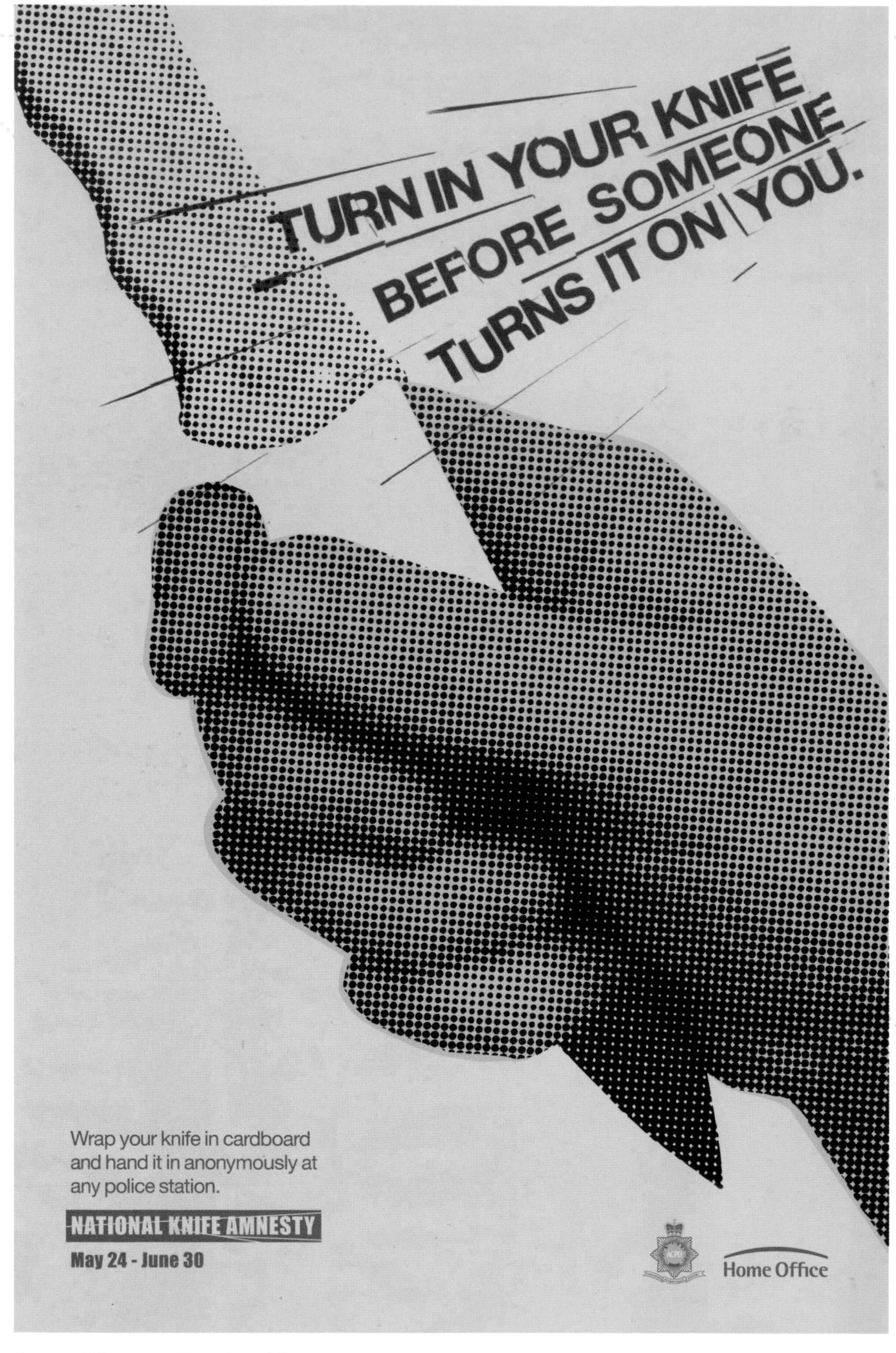

Campaing: Knife Amnesty Client: Home Office

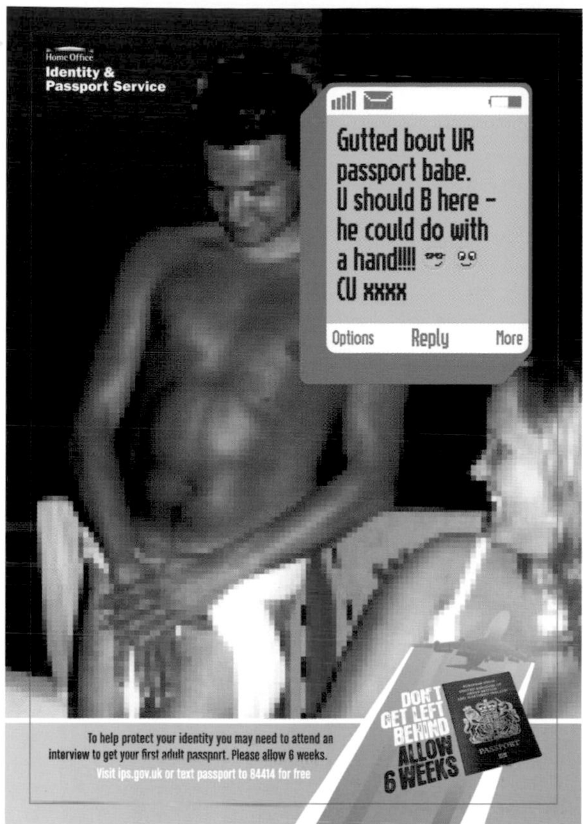

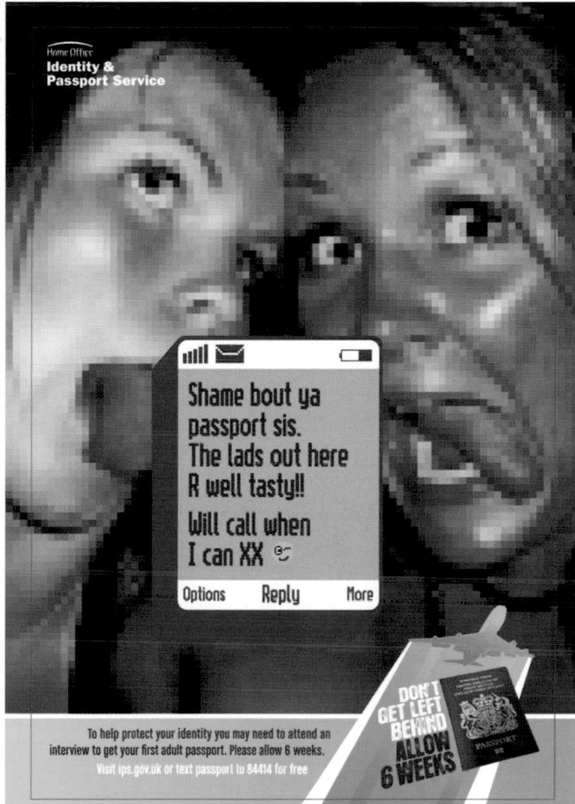

Campaing: 16-24 years olds Passport Application Client: Home Office

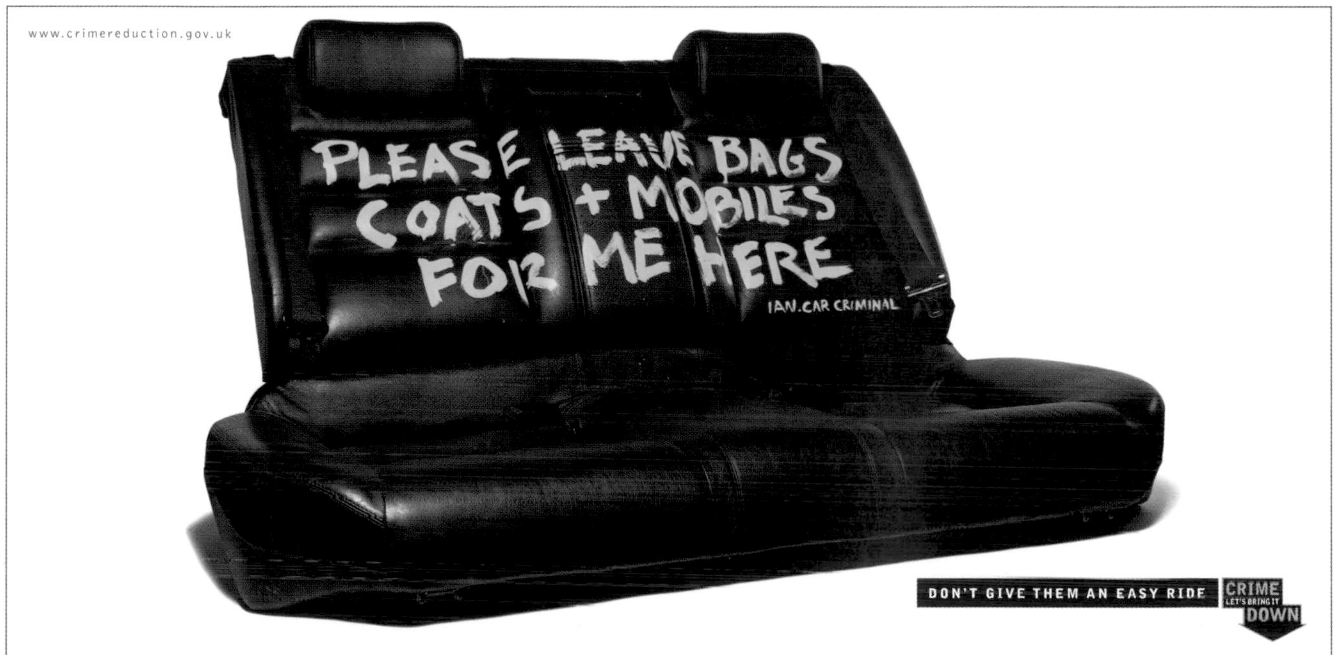

Campaing: Vehicle Crime Reduction Client: Home Office

made to mix with cranberry taste more
BACARDI
SUPERIOR

Campaing: Elixir Client: Bacardi

Bacardi Elixir is more than just an advertising idea. It is a new visual world within which the brand can live. The liquid embodies the characterful taste, warmth and vibrancy of Bacardi, bringing to life the exuberant attitude of those who drink it. Its flexibility has made it relevant on a global basis and the simple creative idea provides the necessary platform to give Bacardi substance, meaning and global resonance.

Strategically:
Many competitor brands focus their strategy on the attributes of the drink itself and others build their positioning around the attitude of the drinkers, but few brands find a solution like Elixir that represents the meeting of the two.

Creatively:
Research demonstrates that the elixir idea has been embrace by consumers as a fresh, innovative and stylish creative approach. The highly visual style enabled us to communicate a breadth of messages without dialogue and at the same time avoid the difficulties of many local advertising restrictions.

Executionally:
We are currently working with an Italian digital company to pioneer a new form of interactive media. Posters and in bar areas will recreate the Elixir idea but will also mimic the movements consumers make in front of it.

Bacardi Elixir es más que una simple idea publicitaria. Es un nuevo mundo visual en el cual la marca puede vivir. El líquido representa el sabor lleno de carácter, la calidez y la vitalidad de Bacardi, sacando a la luz la exuberante actitud de aquellos que lo beben. Su flexibilidad le ha dado importancia a nivel global y una simple idea creativa proporciona el marco necesario para darle sustancia, significado y resonancia global a Barcardi.

Estrategia:
Muchas marcas de la competencia centran su estrategia en las cualidades de la bebida y otros en la actitud de los que la beben, pero pocas marcas encuentran una solución como Elixir, que combina las dos estrategias.

Creatividad:
La investigación demuestra que los consumidores han percibido la idea del elixir como un enfoque creativo fresco, innovador y con estilo. Su estilo altamente visual nos ha permitido expresar varios mensajes sin diálogo y al mismo tiempo evitar las dificultades que suponen las restricciones publicitarias locales.

Ejecución:
Actualmente estamos trabajando con una empresa digital italiana para ser pioneros en un nuevo tipo de medio interactivo. Pósteres y zonas dentro de los bares recrearán la idea de Elixir e imitarán los movimientos que hacen los consumidores cuando lo tienen delante.

BACARDI
SUPERIOR
taste more

BURGER KING
EL ASOMBROSO TOMATE
QUE FUE CASI PARTE DE UN
WHOPPER
LOS INGREDIENTES QUE NO TE GUSTEN
QUE SE BUSQUEN LA VIDA

ZINK project

Zinkproject is a meeting point between the different professionals in the publicity world and the new generation copywriters. Founded by Javier Furones and Natalia Martín, the objective behind Zinkproject is to promote standards of Spanish creativity by introducing Porfolio culture.

In only four years Zinkproject has trained around 400 professionals in areas such as creativity,art management and account executives. Based on the prestigious D&AD workshops, Zinkproject has become place fully adaptable to all the latest communication trends, taking visitors and collaborating with the creative elite.

What better way than for the professionals themselves from the main agencies to train the future generations. In 2007, Zinkproject was the Spanish training centre to receive most awards, its work having been recognised at the majority of nationals and international events such as the One Show, El Ojo de Iberoamerica and CdeC, amongst others.

Zinkproject es un punto de encuentro entre los diferentes profesionales del mundo publicitario y las nuevas generaciones de creativos. Fundado por Javier Furones y Natalia Martín, el objetivo de la fundación de Zinkproject es potenciar los estándares de la creatividad española introduciendo la cultura del Porfolio.

En tan sólo cuatro años Zinkproject ha formado a cerca de 400 profesionales en áreas como creatividad, dirección de arte y Ejecutivos de cuentas. Basado en los prestigiosos workshops del D&AD, Zinkproject se ha convertido en un espacio mudable a todas las nuevas tendencias en comunicación, recibiendo las visitas y colaborando con la élite creativa.

Qué mejor forma que sean los propios profesionales de las principales agencias los que formen a las futuras generaciones. En el pasado 2007 Zinkproject ha sido la escuela más premiada en España, siendo reconocido su trabajo en la mayoría de festivales nacionales e internacionales como el One Show, El Ojo de Iberoamerica y CdeC, entre otros.

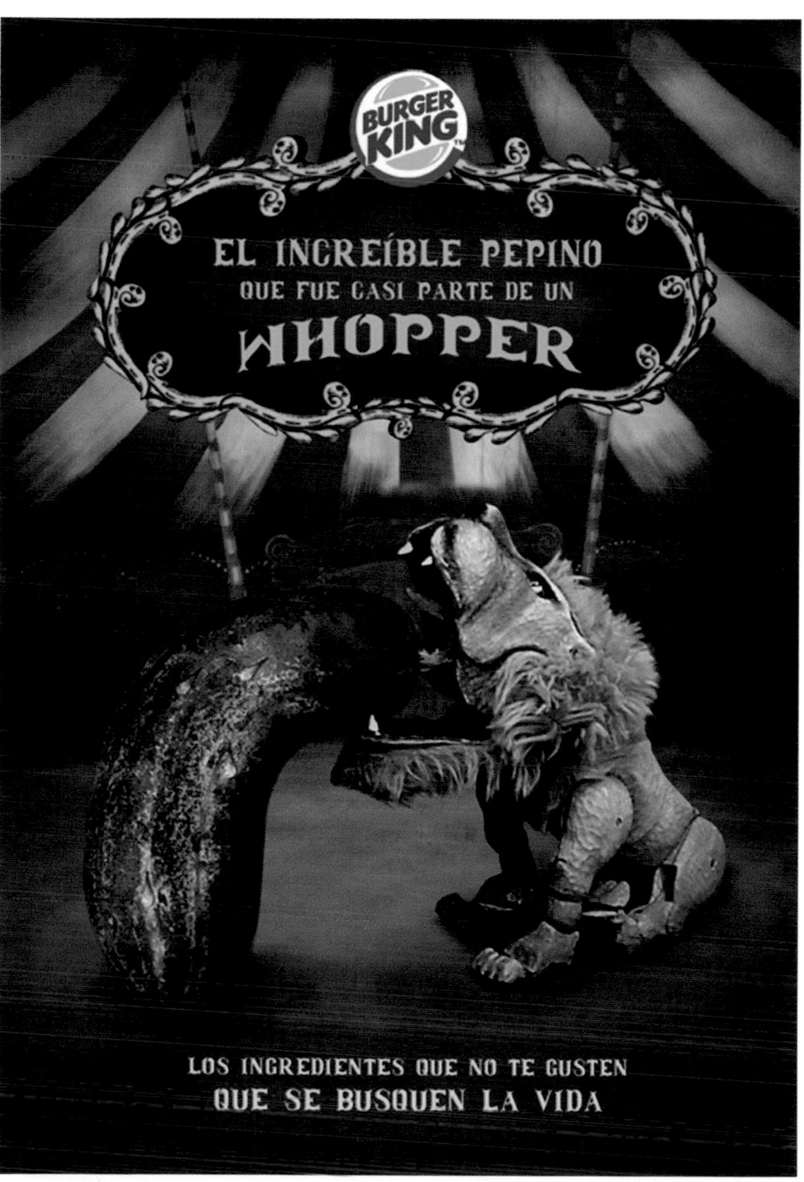

Campaing: Pepino Client: Burger King

Campaing: Tomate Client: Burger King

ESTE CURSO MI PAPÁ ME AYUDA A SACAR MALAS NOTAS

Los abusos sexuales son una carga que el menor lleva siempre consigo y que le impide llevar una vida normal.
En BARNARDOS luchamos para que no haya más niños en esta situación.

Barnardos
NO CHILD GETS LEFT BEHIND
www. barnardos.com

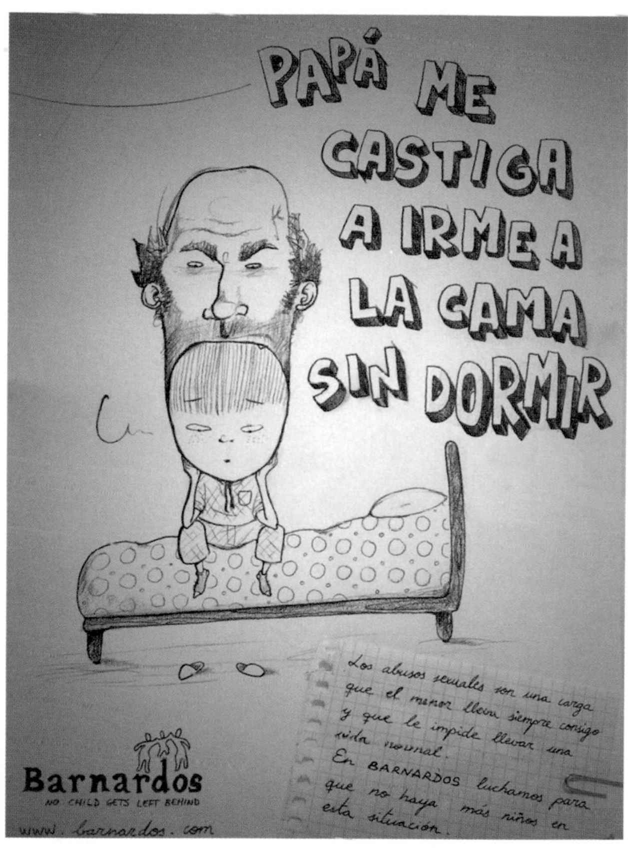

Campaing: Cama, balón, notas Client: Barnardos

The objective of this campaign is to denounce the abuses to minors across a campaign that affects in the problem of a visually very forceful way.

El objetivo es denunciar los abusos a menores a través de una campaña de titulares que incide en el problema de una manera visualmente muy contundente.

Campaing: Bomba Client: Adena

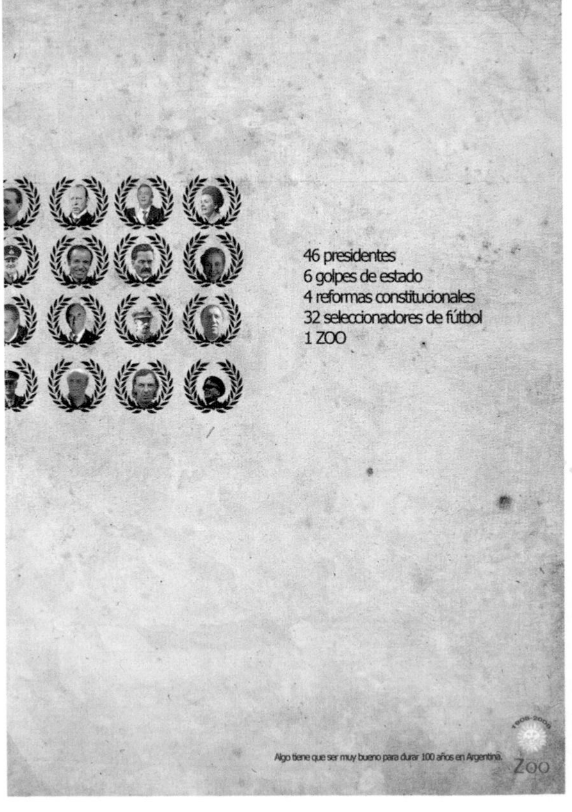

Campaing: Cambios Client: Zoo Buenos Aires

Campaing: Bomba Client: Adena

The objective is to denounce the consequences of the Global Warming, personifying his effects in iconographic forms of destruction, generating a very artistic ambience of terror.

El objetivo es denunciar las consecuencias del Calentamiento Global, personificando sus efectos en formas de destrucción iconograficas, generando una atmósfera de terror muy artistica.

Campaing: Castillo Client: Dunlop

Campaing: Mutantes Client: Dont lose the music

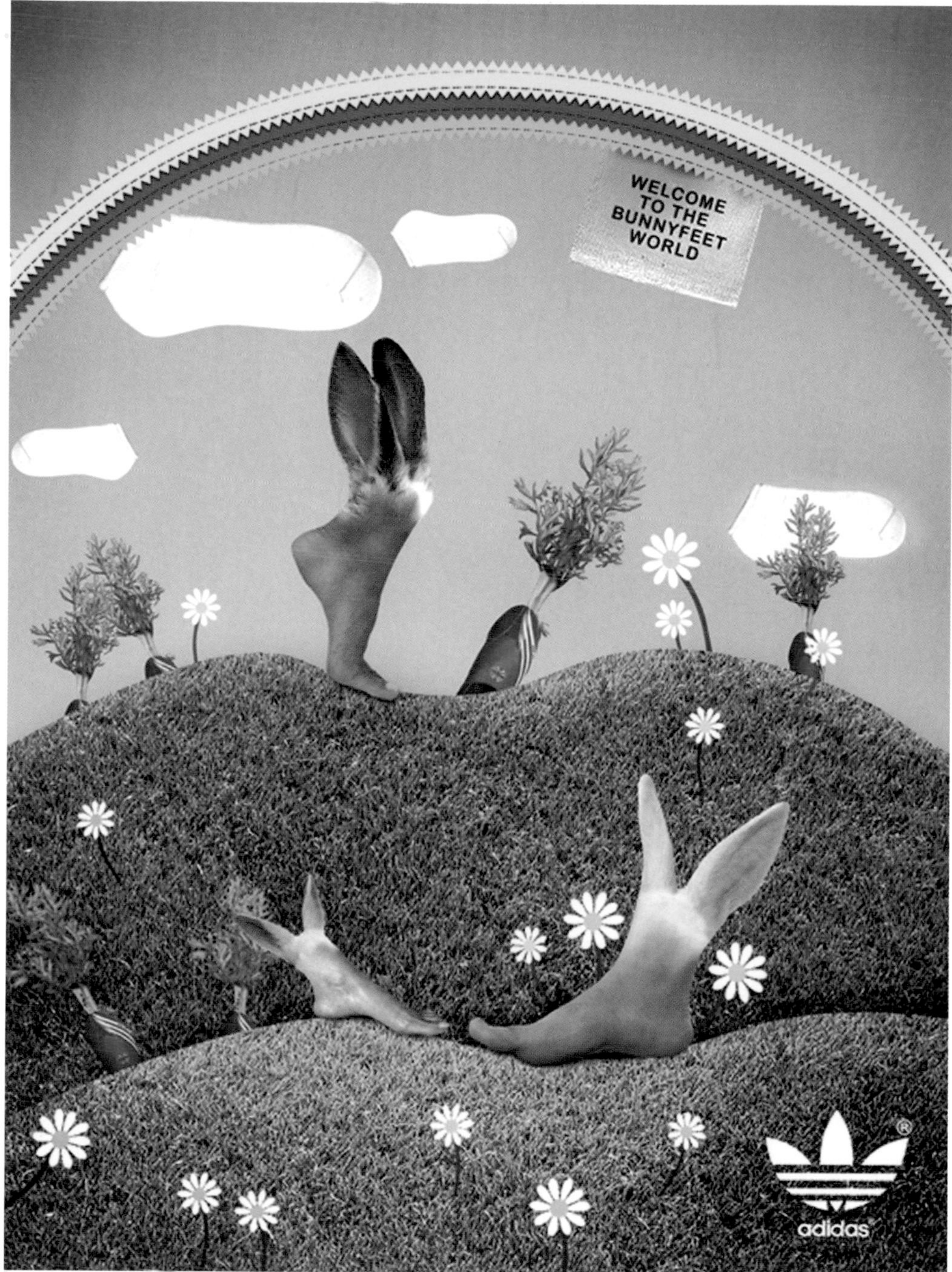

Campaing: Bunnyfeed world Client: Adidas

The objective is to communicate the design of the new sneakers Adidas, transmitting an impressive idyllic world of the "Bunnyfeed".

El objetivo es comunicar las nuevas zapatillas Adidas, trasportandonos a un impresionante mundo idílico de los "Bunnyfeed", "Piesconejo".

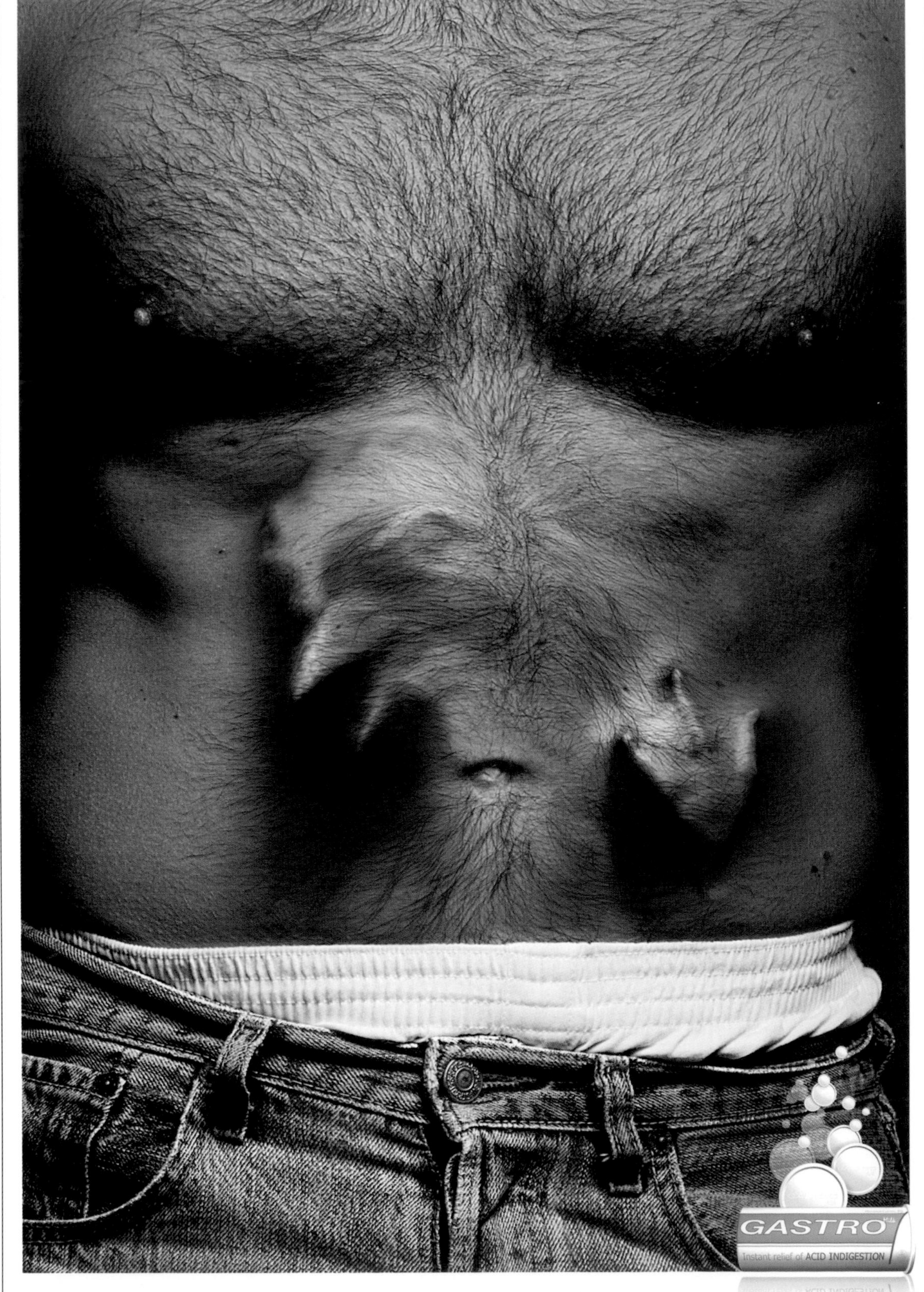
GASTRO
Instant relief of ACID INDIGESTION

grey group

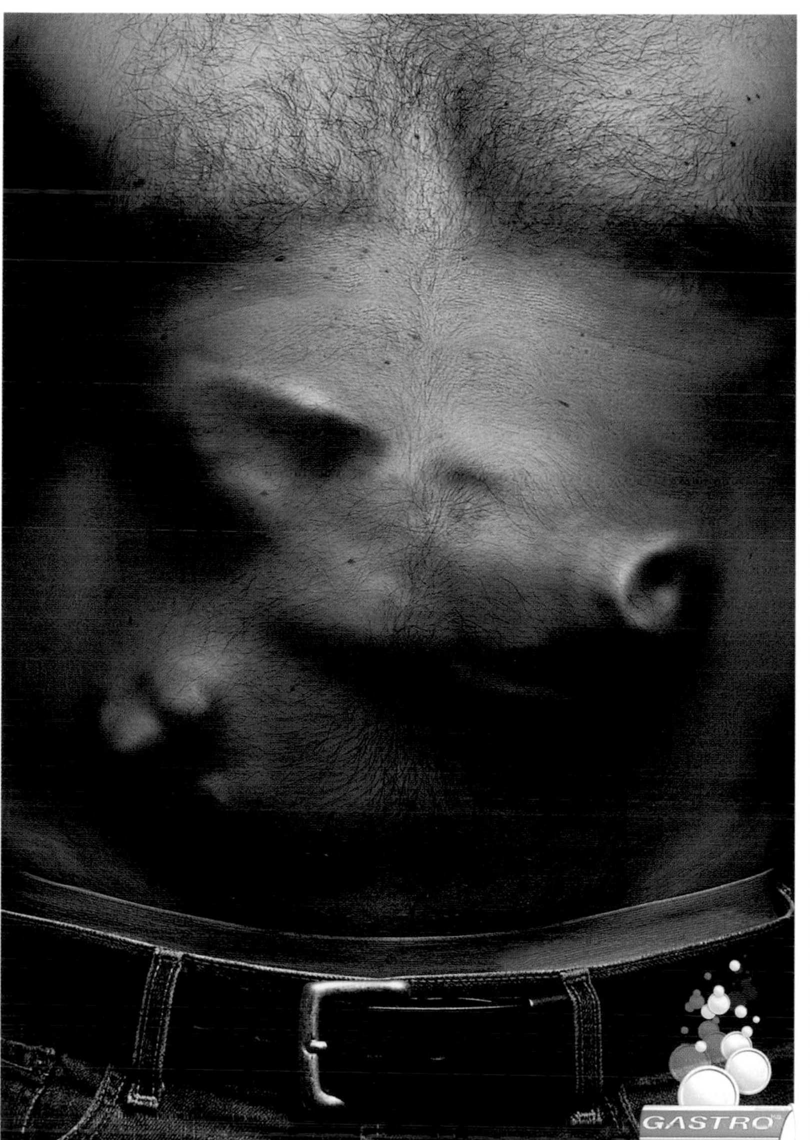

Campaing: Gastro Client: Gastro

Grey Group is a global advertising and marketing agency and a unit of communications conglomerate WPP Group, Grey Global Group was founded in 1917 by Larry Valenstein and Arthur Fatt.

In 1956, Grey acquired its first major client, Procter & Gamble.

Through the 1960s and 1970s, Grey continued to acquire such major accounts, and grew into related communication fields.

In 1988 Grey Communications Group recruited Barry Chapman as Group IS Director.

In 1989 Chapman developed the New Media Experiment. Chapman explored the use of the internet as an alternative to traditional advertising media putting Grey at the forefront of the internet revolution.

Grey Group es una agencia de mercadotecnia, con publicidad global. Agrupa distintas agencias como WPP Group, Grey Global Group.

Grey Group fue fundada en 1917 por Larry Valenstein y Arthur Fatt.

En 1956, Grey adquirió a su principal cliente, Procter & Gamble. Durante los años 1960 y 1970, Grey fue ganando cuentas de grandes clientes, y abarco un amplio mercado en el mundo de la comunicación.

En 1988 el grupo de comunicaciones Grey reclutó a Barry Chapman para que se encargara de la dirección de la empresa.

En 1989 Chapman desarrolló el New Media Experiment, el exploró el uso de internet como nueva alternativa para los medios de la comunicación, dando un salto de la publicidad tradicional, que pone a Grey en la vanguardia de la revolución de internet.

Campaing: 101% Handcrafted Client: Buttero

For Buttero the creative spotlight is always focused on the ability of their craftsmen in making boots perfect down to the last detail and on the fact that every single boot is 100% handmade.

Para la firma Buttero lo más importante es enfocar la publicidad en la capacidad de sus artesanos, en la fabricación de botas perfectas, cuidando hasta el último detalle y destacando que cada bota es el 100 % hecha a mano.

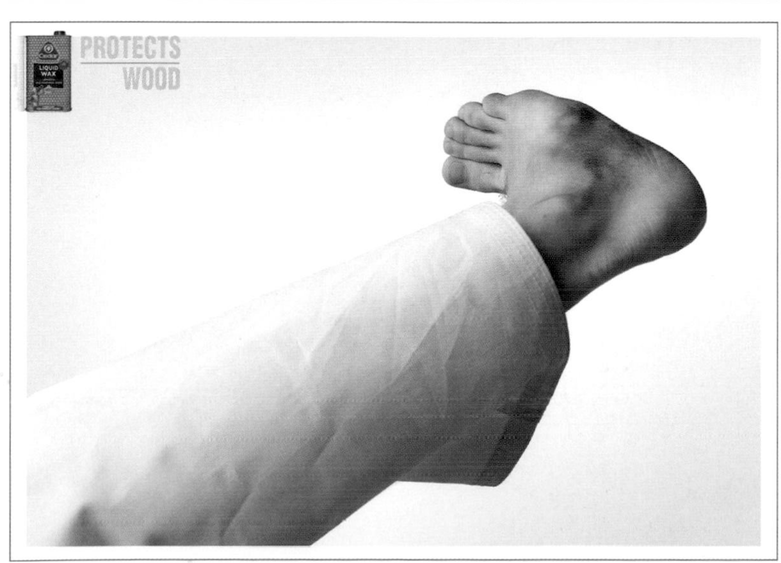

Campaing: Protects wood Client: Ceder

TISSAGES RO CHECHOUART
YANNICK COIF
FEMININ
29

Campaing: Stringfellows Client: Stringfellows

Campaing: Soldman Client: SUNDEK

Campaing: Goodbye Innocence Client: SHS